STRATEGIES

FOR *SERIOUS*

OLDER

ARTISTS

Eric Rudd

D1086425

CIRE

CORPORATION

P U B L I S H E R

North Adams, Massachusetts

CIRE CORPORATION - PUBLISHER
An imprint of Cire Corporation of Massachusetts

Historic Beaver Mill
189 Beaver Street
North Adams, MA 01247-2873 USA

Orders and information: contact@cirecorp.com, or (800) 689-0978

First Printing 2013

Cover: Design by Keith Bona; © Eric Rudd Studio

All photographs © Eric Rudd Studio unless otherwise noted.

Publisher's Cataloging-in-Publication Data
Rudd, Eric.
Strategies for Serious Older Artists/Eric Rudd. –1st ed.
p. cm.
Includes index.
SAN 253-7745
LCCN: 2012953795
ISBN: 978-0-9709959-4-0

1. Art-Vocational guidance. 2. Artists' Estates and Foundations 3. Artists' Studios

I. Title.
N8350.R83 2013   700'.68'2

Preface - Note to the Reader:

This book is an attempt to outline many of the issues involved with working as an older artist and preserving a life's work. However, with hundreds of thousands of possibilities, there is not room to go through every contingency. The author, while experienced, is not a lawyer, accountant, doctor or other licensed expert.

The purpose of this book is to introduce ideas and issues. You are responsible to seek expert advice about all individual cases. The author and the publisher shall have neither liability nor responsibility to any person or entity with respect to any loss or damage caused, or alleged to have been caused, directly or indirectly, by the information contained in this book.

Acknowledgements

In one book, I can't acknowledge all the people who have given me advice and help throughout my career as I now reach senior status.

Foremost thanks go to my wife, Barbara Rudd, who has shared in the struggles and rewards for well over four decades. She has been an active partner in all of this. In part, this book is written and I am practicing what I preach, because I do not wish to dump a collection of my art, greater in number than most museums in the United States, onto her lap if I should predecease her. I also want to thank Barbara for editing this book. Because of my visual mind, I have a strange (and often incorrect) way of verbalizing my thoughts. Without stifling my style, she has attempted to at least correct the most serious of my grammar violations.

I want to thank my sons Thaddeus and Nikolai, now grown, but who grew up with various art experiences; again, I hope they'll have a role but not a liability or burden in preserving my life's work.

I want to also thank Keith Bona, who is a genius designer (for those who see the printed version) and who has given me valuable advice in the production of this book. Keith also suggested that I include the word "Serious" in my title-- it helps to define for whom this book is intended.

Equal thanks go to all the professionals that I've dragged into my problems, and the problems shared by all artists. Believe me, I hope they enjoyed participating because the monetary rewards were slim.

Thanks go also to all the artists whom I've been in contact with over the years; each have put their vision into how they work (a few are mentioned in this book). Now that many of my colleagues are older, I've learned by their examples - good and bad, as I've also explored my options.

TABLE OF CONTENTS

Eric Rudd

Artist Eric Rudd is a well-known sculptor/mixed media artist. Since 1965, Eric Rudd has had numerous one-person and group exhibitions. His work is in many museum and private collections. Originally from Washington D.C., his studio in the Historic Beaver Mill, North Adams, MA is one of the largest private art studios in the United States. He works with new technological processes and materials including robotics, theme-park technology, industrial spray polyurethanes and blow molded polycarbonates. For ten years, he was founder/director of the Contemporary Artists Center, a not-for-profit studio residency and exhibition facility for artists. He is the creator of the Dark Ride Project and A Chapel for Humanity, and co-founded the Center for Robotic Arts at the Massachusetts College of Liberal Arts. He has been the recipient of fellowship grants from the National Endowment for the Arts and the Japan Foundation. He is the author of the books, <u>The Art Studio/Loft Manual - For Ambitious Artists and Creators</u>, <u>The Art World Dream – Alternative Strategies for Working Artists</u>, <u>The Day Something Strange Happened in Sayulita</u>, and the play <u>Wet Paint</u>. He has just completed two novels, <u>The Slums of Heaven</u> and <u>The Circumstances of My Life</u>. www.EricRudd.com.

Introduction

You don't have to agree with all the ideas in this book. You might be convinced that you are still healthy and active and don't have to make any adjustments to your studio routine. You might not care what happens to your art when you are gone. Then again, you might be concerned about how you can continue to create art as you get older, and how your work will be preserved when you are no longer around.

I'm going to show you how to upgrade and adjust your studio methods, how to get ahead of the curve for your later years, and how to preserve your life's work even after you die. I'm going to show you ways to have your own museum space for your work.

You might feel that your work is not there yet, and that it's a bit arrogant to presume your work should have museum space. You might be satisfied with current sales and perhaps your inventory is not building up beyond control.

No matter what you current situation is, I do know that the ideas and problems presented in this book need to be understood as early as possible.

The other thing I know is that there are better systems. The majority of serious working artists accumulate a lot of work, and they should not dump the total outcome of their career to whoever happens to be nearby (spouse, children, close friend) upon their death.

Finally, I know that death is rarely planned-- it could happen tomorrow, or you could live to be 110. But to expect a wonderful old age with sufficient demand for your work so that all your art is preserved and respected - is as unrealistic as worrying about dying tomorrow morning. You have time, although you do need to make plans and take action as soon as possible.

Read all the way through the book before you draw any conclusions about your needs. There are many ideas - some might seem obvious - but you need to assemble all the various issues in your mind before you can make your personal assessment and understand your possible options. I hope you'll be inspired to be as daring as you dream.

The Older Artist

CONGRATULATIONS, YOU QUALIFY FOR AARP

I joke that AARP will send you memberships forms when you turn 40; they don't even wait for the 'official' start age of 50. And before you know it, you'll turn 65 and get those small consolation prizes, like the 10% off at movie theaters or entrance fares. Unfortunately, senior discounts once were more valuable as they really did discount airline fares and hotel rates, for example. Now, online purchases can be made below the official senior fares. I'm afraid that the determents of senior status outweigh the benefits.

Most people think of retirement when they reach their 60s; serious artists don't retire. So are there consequences of continuing to work, often doing very physically hard work, during your later years?

I started showing when I was very young. The art critic for the Washington Post came to the gallery to review my work and to interview me. He wanted to know my age since this was my first one-person exhibition and I had a baby-face; I knew he wanted to write about the "teenager" artist and so I refused to tell him. I wanted to be taken seriously, and I wanted the review - good or bad- to be based on the art and not on me. I had already been the subject of a couple of human-interest articles from previous two-person and group shows, but this review was all about my art. We had a half-hour argument and I finally told him off-the-record (in those days, www.birthdatabase. com or whatever site people use now, didn't exist). Fortunately, I got a good review based on the work, and there was no mention in the article that the art had been created by such a young artist. From that point onward, I never told my age. I later grew a beard to look older because half of my students at the Corcoran (now College of Art) were older than I was. Whenever a museum got one of my works, the date of birth was absent from the label. It was just "Eric Rudd, American."

When did it start to change? I know that fifteen years later, I shaved my beard, and I no longer wanted to seem older-- I wanted to seem younger. I still didn't tell my age (by this time, it had become my idiosyncrasy) but I was neither too young nor too old.

Today, I'm almost embarrassed about my age; I simply don't feel as old as I am. Unfortunately, I'm afraid that people make judgments based on age. If you are receiving social security, you are "over the hill" unless you are famous. I'm active, I'm energetic, and my art is innovative, so I don't want to be put into that box. I feel somewhat more relaxed about my age when I'm with fellow "seniors," but not with the younger artists. I know what it feels like to have someone snub their nose because they think of you like a dinosaur.

At the same time, I've come to realize that the aging process has changed me and does influence my art. I report on the aging effects that will be shared by everyone. This book also acknowledges my transition and what I've done about it. I have realized that there are plans that I need to put into place, should I have an earlier-than-expected demise; and in fact, I have plans in process that will deal with my art after I'm gone. My current projects are perhaps more ambitious than most artists will want for themselves-- but maybe not.

Artists don't like to talk about getting old and the problems that aging brings out. They don't like to talk about what will become of their art, mostly because they've done little about it. Facing these issues has not been fun, but I've found solutions. By coming "clean," I hope I'll help other artists adjust their lives for the better.

BEING OLD- IT'S NOT FUN

90% of adults have vision or hearing loss by the time they qualify for a senior citizen discount. Bones ache, and the body can do less. While Viagra can help some people with transitions in one area, physical deterioration continues internally. Even more essential is how our brains become less sponge like - we don't absorb as much new material as we once did. Dementia and Alzheimer are the two feared words.

Physically, it's tougher to climb stairs or carry heavy materials. A year ago, I decided to paint on traditionally stretched canvas again. I had not done so in two decades. I ended up constructing stretchers and then stretching and priming canvas on over a dozen big canvases, each measuring about 7.5 high x 16 feet wide. Let me tell you, it felt harder to do that work than I had remembered! I'm sure it was as good for me as going to a health club, and I should keep it up for that reason alone, but I can't imagine doing this work in another ten years. Yes, I can hire it out, but again, for those artists who never could afford assistants in the past, why would one expect them to have the income to hire in the future? Normally, we hit our peak at middle age, and then income decreases as we age further.

Then there are the mental and social changes that we notice. My colleagues are dropping like flies. Curators who were once champions of my work (and normally were older than I was as a fresh, hot talent) are now dead, senile or retired. The replacement curators, often in their 20s or 30s, do not get excited to look at the work of someone twice or triple their age. Nor do I blame them. *The world is aimed at what's new and young, not what is aging.* But that doesn't mean that we, the senior artists, don't have feelings. Neglect that increases during our golden years will also cause depression for many artists, as they find themselves forgotten by the fast-moving art world. Most people, and artists are no exceptions, are not prepared for the steady downhill ride, as they get older.

An aging population of artists is growing larger as we live longer than our predecessors. There are an increasing number of people over age 65 who feel pretty healthy and fit and are active. More and more people are living to be 100. Few serious artists ever 'retire' from making art-- they might shift their processes to allow for limitations, but they don't stop making art unless they have no choice. That means that not only do we want to preserve what have made, we also want to support a life-style to allow for future work to be created.

There are more and more pressures on us as our abilities decrease and as our income plummets. For more than a third of the population, social security represents 90% of their income-- obviously for the lower income population. Guess where most artists fit in? Most retirees struggle to just pay the basic bills, but artists lead 'double lives' and have to pay for studio rent and materials as well. Serious artists apply their limited resources far more liberally than retirees who have hobbies. If an artist spends so much for art, there's less for medical, household, and family needs.

Family support often becomes a crucial element as we age, but few family members can deal with the business and quantities of stuff that are common in an active art studio. Usually businesses are sold or handed down upon the owner's retirement, but not so for an art "business." Artists need to continue, despite all the changes and limitations that aging will bring.

WHEN DO YOU NEED TO DO SOMETHING?

Personally, I would prefer to die of old age with my boots on-- so to speak. Go to bed one evening and not wake up in the morning. Unfortunately, death awaits us in a variety of unpleasant ways. So if one were given a terminal diagnosis and had, for argument sake, six months to get your affairs in order, I suppose you might make the argument that there would be sufficient time to determine what was going to happen to your work. But really not, because what you can do in ten years of planning will be far more effective than what you can do in a few months facing death. Then of course, the majority of people will not have that type of advance warning.

In reality, which I tried to suggest in my previous books, the twenty-five year old artist who is just out of art school and beginning a professional art's career, should really be planning for these things from day one. It's no different than thinking about college education for your young children, or putting away money for retirement. The truth is that most art school graduates believe, deep down, that they will be discovered and live like "rock stars" in the not too distant future.

The years go by more quickly than fame develops. And unfortunately, as I've emphasized many times, art schools do not teach the business of being an artist, including real estate, long-term planning and alternative strategies.

Thinking of their young children, parents often will take out an insurance policy in case of unexpected death. These term insurance policies (term policies have no investment value unless they are used upon death) are not expensive and often will have a set premium over twenty years (for example) that won't increase. So for twenty years, if you want to protect your work in addition to your children and spouse, you could consider an additional (or larger) policy aimed at preserving your life's work. But if you live beyond the twenty-year period or the policy expires just as you enter your senior years, a different type of insurance or savings plan is warranted.

Most smart people prepare for retirement years by saving and investing. In a sense, you need to do the same for your work, but in this case, 'retirement' for your art is not just a set period of years to live out, but perhaps becomes an ongoing business that continues after you are dead. After all, your goal and perhaps dream would be to know that your art will continue to be preserved and shown a century into the future. Wouldn't that be satisfying?

There are obvious conflicts if you have a finite amount of money-- family versus your art. If you do things correctly, there should be no question of splitting proceeds. Instead, you'll need to double your efforts and results in order to reach a satisfying goal of protecting your family as well as your art. You'll also need to know the various strategies that are open to you.

THE CONCEPTS AND PROBLEMS THAT NEED TO BE ADDRESSED

I wrote two books, <u>The Art World Dream - Alternative Strategies for Artists</u> and <u>The Art Studio/Loft Manual - For Ambitious Artists and Creators</u> about a dozen years ago; both books are still relevant and do address some of the ideas that I'll be discussing in this book. But as artists get older, concerns increase and/or change about how to work or what art to focus on, getting known, preserving one's art, and what really will happen to our life's art/work when we die.

Ok, we can take the easy method, unfortunately preferred by the vast majority of artists. Simply die and let the family worry about it. You'll be dead and there's probably not much you can do about things anyway-- right? Nonsense! There's a lot you can do and it's really irresponsible to drop this onto family and friends.

Who am I addressing this to? Well, I am assuming that if you are a serious artist, that you have been working and creating art (or collecting art), and unless you are a handful of fortunate ones who have achieved so much success that you are sought after by museums and you have auction value, my guess is that you have accumulated a lot of art - and that art is at risk upon your death.

Personally, the grass is always greener in someone else's studio. A realist painter, for example, like a Chuck Close, might only create a dozen original paintings a year. With multiple works on paper, the total outcome - even if most are not sold - do not take up a lot of space. The total production over 50 years might not add up to more than 500 paintings. That's manageable, especially if many have been sold along the way. (And of course, anyone with a name like "Chuck Close" does not have to worry - museums will be scrambling to get his work.)

Artists who are more productive on an annual basis, however, might now have works numbering in the thousands. You might have stacks and stacks filled with paintings. If you have the "misfortune" to have pursued a career in sculpture, your problems multiply greatly. Sculptures might be larger, heavier, harder to store, more fragile, made of various materials and in parts -- all far more complex than 'traditional' art on canvas.

In my own case, for example, I have large sculptures numbering more than a hundred - at least! When I think about any specific work, I have no idea how to get it out of my studio and into a secure home. Most of them would fill an entire average room; in the decades since I produced most of them, I have not been able to sell those giant ones, nor even give them away to a reputable institution. Why would anyone want them after I die? I had to purchase an industrial mill just to have the space to store them; not many people have the type of space to accommodate "elephant-sized" artwork.

Just a couple of the hundreds of "elephant-sized" sculptures and reliefs in my studio. Who will take responsibility for these after the artist's death?

Then there are installation and conceptual artists whose works are difficult simply due to technology used and the need to assemble perhaps hundreds of elements.

For any and all of the above, there is also the need to think about archival materials, whether these are models, sketches, notes, letters, diagrams, photos, slides, digital records, past sale records, and relevant papers. Certainly if your name was "Picasso," all that stuff would be eagerly sought after by curators hoping to shed light on how these masterpieces came about and the personal history of the artist.

I don't want to forget about art collectors who, slowly at first but over decades, have accumulated hundreds of works of art. Unless the collection is one of a small number with art that museums will be waiting with open arms to accept, you might be loaded with dozens if not hundreds of quality artists who simply do not have the name status (i.e. auction value) that will allow you to easily find a new home.

I've known artists who have achieved a national reputation, who even have had auction value (i.e. they are sought by museums) and still they pay plenty of rent for storage space, especially for their early work. Few artists sell their entire production. Museums can only take so much. The good news for artists with large reputations is that upon death, there is a commercial value to their work that would attract dealers or appointed executors to invest the time and effort to get them sold or placed.

A TYPICAL TRAGIC STORY

Let me give you a tragic case to demonstrate what I'm talking about. There was a New Jersey artist who was active, exhibited regionally and even had a few inclusions in New York group museum shows. When he died, he left his daughter a total of 1,700 paintings and works on paper, with a few sculptural reliefs and other oddities. The artist's late wife had also been an artist, and there was an assortment of her works thrown into the mix.

The daughter rented a studio from me of 1,000 square feet, in part I believe, because she thought she could tap into other artists who were renting in the same building for help in sorting through the piles of works - photographing them and doing archival work. She ended up renting the space for ten years making very little progress with archival work, nor in getting then sold or distributed. And then she passed away.

Now it ended up in the granddaughter's lap. To her credit, she came over one day with a U-Haul truck and took away about 200 works. What happened to the rest? You can guess -- all into the dumpster, as she vacated the rental studio and reduced the financial strain.

The studio was a bargain - with little heat being use, I charged her a discounted rental of only $300 a month. That's a ridiculously tiny amount compared to space in most big cities, but even at this rate, times ten years, that was more than $36,000 invested for no results. In the end, most of the art was thrown away.

The truth is that most art made by the majority of artists will end up in the attic, basement, dumpster or flea market.

That's the reality and that's why I wrote this book.

I offer some suggestions and solutions, but I wrote much of this book simply to make you aware; I can do that more easily since I am sharing with you my own frustrations and issues - and how I'm dealing with it all. The solutions are out there, but time is an enemy, especially when we finally realize what we need to do, but we don't have the time left or resources to do it all.

Aging and Working

OUR PREDECESORS

Tour any large art museum of European Renaissance art, and you'll see that the majority of paintings and sculptures on display were created when the artists were younger than 40. That's because artists started training as apprentices early in their teens, and because people didn't live as long.

Youthful creativity seems to have general advantages, as some of the greatest discoveries and art movements have been instigated by young scientists and artists. Einstein and Picasso are the first to come to mind. Picasso changed the world of art while still in his 20s.

There are exceptions and there are many examples of great art being produced in later years. Matisse with his collages and Monet with his Water Lilly paintings are obvious examples. Louise Bourgeois and Georgia O'Keeffe created masterpieces in their 90s. And there are scores of major artists still doing museum-worthy art in their 70s and 80s and older. Because we are living longer and because there are more artists working today than ever before in history, more and more masterpieces will be created by seniors.

The flame need not go out; often, artists with reputations and therefore with financial ability or large commissions can realize some of their monumental goals. Many of us have the feeling to slow down a bit, only because quantity becomes less of a concern and the chance to do some of the 'big' works seem more important. As I think about my almost five decades of work, I mentally click on my favorites - my 'masterpieces' - and I'd like to have a few more of them. I care less about producing quantity; I'd rather work on one big work (i.e. important, not to say that size determines that) than half a dozen smaller ones.

In some ways, the mature years are the time to assess what are the new works or projects that you want to do and to then concentrate on them.

THE LIMELIGHT LEAVES YOU

Just as curators won't necessarily call you as often, neither will you have as many party invitations. You might hanker down with your small group of friends, but you'll be more and more relegated to the background as the art scene moves on. There are exceptions; if you have a reputation, you might be rediscovered and name recognition has proven value, but that's probably one artist out of a thousand.

I live in a small town where I was the "one-man band" doing just about everything. I'm still active, but in the past decade, I've been joined by two or three hundred artists who have moved here. Most are younger, and they have their own scene. I'm known, but just not a part of every art-related thing that's going on like I used to be. And it also has to do with the fact that I voluntarily stepped back or stepped aside to let the new energy do things, whether it's to organize downtown exhibitions, support new alternative spaces, operate the new arts program at the college, get artists excited about open-studio events, or arrange for tours of artist lofts-- if you aren't the one up to your ears doing it, you'll naturally not be included in the fun parts-- dinner meetings, receptions, openings, and so forth. As I said, all this is natural, but it is very typical for senior artists to just be less active within their profession. Couple this with how new curators look for new talent, and I've noticed frustration on the part of many of my senior colleagues.

There are ways to adjust. If you think what you are doing is more important than ever in your life, then you'll brush aside these rejections and in the end, what you accomplish creatively will win the day.

LIFE IS EASIER TODAY

When you think about how it was when we were young, life is much easier now. For example, is it really necessary to physically visit an art store anymore? You can order anything online and UPS will deliver it to your door - within a day if you need something fast. More and more eateries and grocery stores have delivery service and prepared meals. Books and magazines can be purchased and downloaded electronically. Even movies now come to you directly to your computer and television.

Depending on processes, much more can be purchased ready-to-use. Because of world markets, goods are cheaper than ever. For example, for one oddball project, I needed 420 stretched canvases, 24 x 30 inches. In the old days, that would have been quite a studio undertaking - getting the lumber, cutting it to length, assembling the parts, cutting and stretching the canvas and then priming it. It might have been so much work that my idea might not have ever been realized. But now life is easier and faster. For less money than I could even buy the raw lumber, a Vietnamese manufacturer fabricated the canvas, then sent it to a Chinese factory that stretched and primed the canvas onto built stretchers, then shrink-wrapped them with retail labels and shipped them to the United States where a company (in this case I purchased from Dick Blick because they had a sale going on, but other companies also carry them, like Utrecht, for example) sold the canvases to me and shipped them to my door for a bargain price of $5.40 per canvas, and they still made a profit! Unbelievable. Like I said, I couldn't buy the lumber for one stretcher at a nearby lumberyard for $5.40. Yes, there are political issues involved with outsourcing, but nevertheless, materials are available cheaper than ever before. In the same way that you can purchase many materials at great discounts, a few dollars can keep me supplied for years. If you read The Art World Dream, you'll learn about other ways to get materials at quantity for peanuts.

Discounts like I describe might make a critical difference as resources, energy and income dry up in your later years. It sounds like a non-issue, but often I've had ideas that I've passed on because I didn't want to waste the extra money. Thank goodness that I had foresight. For example, I must have 10,000 sheets of paper and still more in rolls. If I didn't have this supply, and I had to purchase new paper for one or two dollars a sheet, I might not do the stuff on paper that I now do. Most older artists do tighten up on their expenses; it's human nature and it affects their studio output.

As artists shift their processes upon aging, for instance, making models that might be enlarged into giant sculptures by others rather than undertaking the sculptures themselves, or (like Matisse) cutting up paper shapes while in bed for an assistant to attach to a large panel - limitations can also become opportunities.

There are sculptors who have changed styles in order to cease using dangerous materials. After a number of years, one begins to think about the consequences more and more. I sprayed polyurethane foam for 35 years. Although I used a fraction during any given year compared to someone using the materials daily doing commercial applications, nevertheless, I figured I had been exposed enough. Even with masks and gloves and the best I could afford for ventilation and exhaust systems, I wonder how much got into my system and how much damage might have occurred. Although I miss the 'action,' enough was enough.

Whether it's chemical exposure, physical strength diminishing, size and weight consideration - often decisions to change artistic concepts are a disguise for changes required by aging. Older artists often can't continue the way they worked decades earlier, just as athletes have to decrease their activities and accept lower results.

AGING - ECONOMICS

Let me spend just a brief time talking about aging and economics generally. If we are lucky, we will all go through this life phase and there are many agencies, books, advisors and so forth to help. Programs that support seniors in any field will also help artists, of course.

The most significant two pieces of support for U.S. senior citizens are social security payments and Medicare.

I'm not an economist or tax advisor, but the basic decision for social security is whether to take benefits as soon as one qualifies, or to wait. The longer you wait, the higher the monthly stipends will be. Very generally, if you take benefits at age 62 rather than wait until you are 70 years old, you will be ahead of the game until you reach (approximately) 80 years of age. At that point, the higher monthly benefits will surpass the money you've taken in for the eight years. Now whether you use this money or save it and invest it will make a difference, as well as what your tax rate is for this income. If you defer receiving benefits until 70 and you die before you are 80, you lose the game (in money terms). If you live past 80, you win. That's it in a nutshell but the exact numbers/ years will vary. Some say, "A bird in hand," and others say, "If you don't need it, wait." Also, stay tuned as Congress may tinker with this formula anyway.

Nevertheless, with age, you will receive some financial security in the form of social security deposits, which you can arrange to be direct-deposited electronically into your checking or savings bank account. At age 65, the other significant economic change will be a huge deduction in expenses, namely for health insurance. While you might elect to purchase a supplemental (gap) policy that will pay you for whatever Medicare won't pay, the premium for this insurance is a fraction of the cost of full fledge medical insurance.

For example, earning $10,000 (it could be a lot more) in social security and saving $10,000 in insurance premiums, equal a $20,000 swing in your annual budget-- that's significant for many artists.

If one were forward thinking enough to have purchased residential and studio space early on, at least in your 40s, then by this Social Security age, your property would be paid off and all mortgage payments would end as well. This might add another $10,000 to $20,000 saving.

And of course, by this time, college payments for children have been completed, and perhaps benefits from a partner/spouse will double the earnings and savings.

Combining these factors can allow smooth sailing for many folks. However, these are just very general numbers and life usually is much more complicated.

IT TAKES A SCARE

I had a medical scare a while back. Basically a false alarm- I'm still here, but it got me asking myself, "How prepared am I?"

Like many artists, I have a lot going on. I have bills for my residence, plus studio and art related expenses. I have various business accounts and for each account, there's a separate user name and password. My life seems littered with access codes.

More than once, I showed my wife where the list of accounts was located, and she nodded. But that's not the same as taking over, using these accounts and paying the bills and making sure the income continues. What I showed her a year ago evolves constantly and even so, I wonder how good her memory will be if she really did need to deal with it all. Showing her a list once a year or so simply isn't adequate.

My scare made me realize that most of my preparations were in my head. Only I knew where all the papers and checkbooks were in the desks, where things were filed, where account numbers and access codes were kept, how to use the online bill paying systems, and so forth. In all actuality, I think a transition would be a mess. I take care of all the bills and income, and my wife handles just some medical bills and donations. She wouldn't easily be able to fill my shoes; after all, I've been doing this for decades. And why would I want to burden her down with all the work I now do? As an artist, I volunteer to work until death; but my spouse is in her retirement mode, not work mode. So while some work continues for all of us, there is a balance that most people want as they get older.

Just because I should drop dead, the mailman would not stop delivering bills the next day and they still would still be due. Mortgages or loans, utilities, credit cards - all have to be paid, and in our case because we lease space in order to achieve large studio space, rents have to be collected, leases renewed, spaces rented and maintenance continued.

Fifteen years ago, my father asked if I would take over his finances if he should become incapacitated or upon his death. My mother was not capable of dealing with the business aspects. So he made lists for me, and we went over them on several visits. About two or three years later in his early 90s and a couple of years before his death, his mental abilities diminished and I had to take over completely. As it turned out, I also had to make changes. He had accounts all over the place, many small ones, including tiny insurance policies completely paid up so that upon his death, they would pay the same as just cashing them in early. It was far easier to do those things while he could sign documents, than to do those things afterwards. I ended up taking all his investments and accounts and consolidated them into one account under one brokerage/banking roof. I opened up a new bank account at my bank, and all accounts were linked so I could handle them all online.

I learned a lot about simplifying and consolidating and expediting from this process. I also learned how vulnerable old people are. I can't tell you how many people, from legit to semi-legit or crooked businesses to even family members, have tried to take advantage of my mother (who as I write is now 99 years old). I'm certain that if I had not been around, she would be broke now. But not everyone has the financial experience to do this - for an aging parent and later, for themselves. I wonder if anyone will be able to do for my wife and me as much as I've done for my parents.

If I should predecease my wife, although she's bright and has handled plenty of business matters over the years, I'm not sure she could readily take over, nor would she want to. But my medical scare reminded me that something could happen to me at any moment. If I had a real medical issue that needed my attention, I'm not sure what frame of mind I'd have (assuming I had that much advance warning) to go through a complete training.

These concerns are just for regular income and expense issues. Then there are all my art concerns. Who will know where everything is, what's important and what is not, where to start, and who to draft to help? Even such small things as web site domains have to be renewed-- they might be critical in the long run. But I haven't taken out 10-year domain; I usually renew them every two years. Should I start to think differently? Should I do a dry-run, and pretend I'm a goner in a few months and put into place a written action plan covering all that I think is critical to continue operations, and all that I think is important for my art? Certainly every time I go up in an airplane, these thoughts reoccur.

Then, too, I think about my survivors' needs. Will my spouse someday want to move on and have her own life without me? I'm assuming the same love and attention as we give each other now --- but life doesn't work like that. Will our adult children have emergency needs that I can't anticipate? No one wants to really think about these things but then again, to continue to be blind about what will actually and eventually happen is to be irresponsible.

I don't want to spend a disproportionate amount of time on this. How many fire drills are necessary? On the other hand, I'm juggling so many balls in the air, some sort of adequate plan and instructions should be made available to an estate lawyer and to reliable family members just in case.

AGING- PHYSICAL

As aging diminishes our physical capabilities, where and how we work must be considered. As will be mentioned later in detail, residing and working in a community condominium loft building, rather than having a house with separate studio, might eliminate most of the maintenance headaches and allow for easier workspace.

Downsizing in other ways, moving to an easier climate, moving closer to your needs - any of these things can make your life generally easier. These options might become necessary, or might be desirable if you plan in advance for them.

No matter how much one reduces the physical strain in the studio, it is equally important to keep up with activity to keep oneself fit. The old adage that you need to either use it or lose it is appropriate. Taking your vitamins, eating healthy foods and avoiding quantities of sugar and fat, getting exercise regularly even by walking, staying mentally active and involved-- all these things will help the average person age gracefully and allow that person to keep youthful enough to continue making art. At the same time, changing habits so that accidents are avoided is a smart thing to start with. Whether it's not climbing ladders, or lifting heavy materials or breathing dangerous odors or using tools without proper eyewear (and using glasses for better sight) - any and all these precautions might make a difference.

Finally, a doctor once told me that men should not die from prostate cancer or colon cancer. In other words, these are preventable deaths if men get annual checkups and regular colonoscopies. Women should check their breasts regularly and have annual checkups as well. Many diseases can now be controlled or lessened if they are caught early. I know quite a few artists of both sexes who seem to have a lackadaisical attitude about their health.

DEPRESSION IS COMMON BUT RARELY ARTISTS ARE DEPRESSED WHEN THEY ARE SUPER PRODUCTIVE

I don't clean my studio as often as I should, but that's a necessary task in preparation for new work. I arrive at the studio and just the thought of spending an entire day physically cleaning or doing functional preparation work, like building stretchers or stretching canvas, causes me to hesitate about doing new work. It's a stupid reason, I know better than anyone, yet if I were to admit the truth to you, I would have to make this confession. I feel like I'm lazy but in reality, it's just because my energy level is not where it was when I was twenty years old. Instead, I need to focus my energy on new work rather than maintenance or prep work, before I run out of steam. If I waste it on cleaning or maintenance chores, I lose my energy to make new art and I feel like I'm falling behind.

Just to admit this out loud is almost like being at an AA meeting. Once recognized, these issues need to be part of your new plan to deal with your art-- and that means dealing with current storage and maintenance issues in addition to current or future art projects.

Not maintaining the level of my art production tends to depress me. Rarely have I been depressed when I've been busy in the studio. Art always excites me, except for the laborious processes-- but as I see a vision come into reality, my excitement takes over. However, if I face too much before I can get into the creative end, I'll tend not to realize the idea; failure to make art is a sure formula for depression.

Aging normally triggers depression for a variety of reasons, usually to do with diminishing abilities, being forgotten by family, friends, colleagues and in an artist's case, by gallery and museum officials. Seeing your friends and associates die off is not a fun occurrence.

Some artists prosper in their later years, success building upon success, but for many, their careers go in the opposite direction. Also true is the fact that almost all artists want more. A museum director used to tell me how some of the biggest names imaginable used to complain constantly. If they were offered a retrospective at the Whitney, they'd complain it wasn't at the MoMA. Or they'd complain that the museum wasn't spending enough on the catalog, or publicity, or something. Most artists I know only dream of an opportunity like that; it's hard to believe that one would complain, but the tendency to want more never seems to go away.

So as artists get into their senior years, any frustration only seems to increase, in one's mind. Then if there are other worries, like health or money or relationships, the artist can be in a very fragile state.

I like to say that my sense of humor has carried me through many rough times, but not everyone has developed this shield.

WE CAN TEACH OLD DOGS NEW TRICKS

There are two aspects of this thought - one is that artists don't want to change their approach to art as they mature. The other aspect is that aging mandates new processes simply because we can't do what we once did.

Even late in life, it's necessary to sit back and take a far-view perspective of where you've been and where you are going. But stubbornness is a trend with older people. They are set in their ways and to change sometimes implies that their views are no longer valid.

Good artists should be more resistant to narrow vision and stubbornness than the general population. Most people want calm lives and routines. Artists, however, are constantly questioning, challenging and destroying part of their art during the creative process in order to realize something greater. So with that ability in the studio, it is a shame that often they don't apply the same determination in how they structure their lives.

Aging will make changes more difficult because we all get used to things. But if you read this book and then sit down and examine your lifestyle carefully, and apply the same process to it as you would in creating your art, you will find new solutions and new options.

Even for me, it's hard to keep up with new technologies like the younger generation in their twenties. That's not to say it's all out of reach. I find it sad when I see too many older artists working or administrating like they were in the dark ages-- and that 's coming from someone who gets funny remarks from my sons. I don't watch enough TV to stimulate me investing in devices to record and play back various shows that I might have missed while being out. I am also not into rearranging play lists to play on our iPod, although our son, who is in the music business, did download for us a few thousand songs. Nevertheless, I am into saving myself time in doing chores that have to be done.

I have considered myself an unexpected expert in two aspects of art - how to realize ambitious dreams in a realistic way, and how to economize and become more efficient in those processes that have to be done. In other words, I can apply my mind to outrageous art visions as well as apply my mind to how I go about doing the mundane stuff that is either necessary to live or necessary to realize my art goals.

If you are reading this on your Kindle or iPad, you probably are pretty current with technology, but you'll be surprised to know how many older artists are not. I can tell just from casual observation.

Most people do use computers but many senior artists barely do more than write emails or surf the web to do some shopping. That's a start but you need to use technology to save time and effort.

If you have a studio, you are probably paying more bills than someone who is employed at a company and just has household expenses. I have a long list of bills, because I also help a couple of family members and that was using up hours of my time. Using online bank services allows you to pay bills without writing a check, or buying a stamp and envelop. You can write a check to anyone, for free. What used to take me two hours or more per month now takes me 15 minutes, and I save a few hundred dollars per year in avoiding mailing supplies. That's a real difference. If you aren't doing this now, it's an indication that you are not optimizing the necessities in your life. And you should start today!

Email has become essential for me, as I respond quickly to dozens of messages that come in daily. I have no patience for Facebook but I understand that I really should add that to my routine if I want to gather support for my large projects. Facebook is taking the place of business web sites for many. For years, letter writing via email has become an essential way that I go and seek favors and support for my projects. It has resulted in residencies and free manufacturing access and free materials worth hundreds of thousands of dollars. The rewards are there for those who ask.

For those who do their own accounting to some degree, Quickbooks ™ or a similar accounting program is essential and the quickest way to keep track of all your financial records. Once you learn the routine, it becomes fast and mechanical. A no-brainer, as they say.

Even household chores, and possibly studio chores can be done for less money and effort. A robotic vacuum does an incredibly good job (you'll know because when you dump the dirt compartment after the initial runs, you'll see how much was picked up; the more you vacuum, the less there'll be). So you push a button and go to the bed or leave the studio or house. Simple. And the cost is no more than for an average vacuum. They have a 'shop vacuum' version that will also take care of studio debris. (You'll still need to have a powerful shop vacuum for those bigger piles.)

Obviously, scanners, and cheap printers can save a trip to the copy store. These devices are also invaluable as you begin to keep new digital records of your art and office files.

Even I resisted a cell phone when they first become affordable, but by the end of the first day when I used one, as I was standing on a roof and needing an answer for the roofer, I saved myself a trip down to a land phone or to the lumberyard. I was a convert. Now with the iPhone, the services are invaluable, with GPS maps, messages, email, camera, and many apps available for free.

Do I need the next generation of my phone? Of course not; perhaps if I were 20 years old and in the thick of things I would upgrade annually, but I'm not. Nevertheless, I do want to save time and save effort. As the cost of new technology has plummeted, it is more than foolish not to be current with the basic versions.

At the same time, the flip side is to not put so much importance on technology that you lose sight of the real thing. I used to be critical of artists who spent too much time fine-tuning their bio's to submit to galleries and designing their business cards. Making good art will carry the day- not what your resumes or business cards look like.

I say the same thing about web sites. We all have them and I'm guilty because I don't update my own. I use it to give some basic information and ways to contact me. I've known artists who have spent thousands of dollars on them and they are still out-of-date a year later. Plus, more importantly, unless you are producing a popular product, they don't do that much good, except for the artist's ego. It's an introduction, that's all. A web site is not the 'end all.'

FLORIDA JOKES

"It's so much fun to be reintroduced to your best friends."
   -or-
"Why did you marry her at your age? Is she pretty?
"No."
"Can she cook?"
"No. "
"Then why?"
"Because she can drive at night."

The jokes continue about old age, but you know, some of them come too close to the truth for comfort. So we make adjustments. But in art, these adjustments become critical on helping us to continue our output.

I don't worry about needing walkers or wheelchairs, but I did think early on, when I was primarily a painter, that if were ever injured in an accident, I could build a grid with lift, so I could reach any height or left-right direction and I could continue to paint on wall-sized canvases. Of course, an assistant would be on the floor getting the paint colors ready for me to apply.

As I age, these ideas often return, as I see devices that can make creating art more accessible even for someone who might have diminished capabilities. Lifts of many styles are part of many contractor businesses' standard equipment, wheelchairs have become much more sophisticated and powered to do all kind of movements, robotic arms are now economically affordable, and power tools are the norm, not the odd exception.

Artists need to see what's now acceptable equipment and processes, and not become a joke; the joke is not funny when it prevents the artist from creating his or her best.

The Studio; Now and Later, and perhaps...

MAKE THE ADJUSTMENTS TO YOUR STUDIO OPERATIONS NOW

Keeping in mind that you aren't going from very active to cripple overnight, there are still operational changes that would be smart to make, even while you are currently fit.

Think about the operational end of your studio, as if it were a business. Are there cheaper ways to do things? Can you outsource work to regional or even overseas contractors? Can you purchase quantity goods at discount, and then set up a delivery system within your studio so every time you need something it is not a big deal?

Some things are tiny-- and may even seem stupid to mention, but you know, it all adds up. For example, most artists wouldn't hesitate to climb a ladder to change a light bulb. The problem is, I've known artists who stopped climbing ladders only after an accident, not when the aging body was hinting to them to stop. Can one make the lighting cheaper and needing to be changed less frequently? Of course - with the long-life bulbs. I have a relative who owned a lighting business for many years, and he mostly serviced big-box stores, but the principle is the same- it's too expensive to change each bulb when it goes out. It's cheaper to understand the life expectancy and to go in and change all the bulbs at the same time, with the work scheduled when the store is closed. New bulbs and fixtures are more economical to run, and they shine brighter. What's good for the big-box store is good for a studio. And it's not all about money; it's about your well-being. Changing to longer-life, lower wattage usage bulbs, and then having someone else replacing them all at once is a good way to avoid having to climb a ladder to change a bulb when you shouldn't be doing that kind of thing. A fall from a ladder at age 70 is far different than falling at age 40.

Again, these are small things, but you could make a list of a hundred such examples, even within an average size studio. A five-minute irritation is nothing in your prime, but they take on added weight as senior citizens. But no matter the age, I've always taken an interest in making the fabrication end of my art easier and cheaper-- it allows me to do more and to put more concentration onto the art aspect. That starts with getting quantity art supplies at a fraction of the retail price. Once I have them, I store the supplies to make them available when I need them. And then I try to use the materials in a process that is as efficient as I can make it, so that whatever effort I want to put into the creative end is not hampered by the preparation process.

To realize new forms, I've had to turn to new technologies and space-age materials such as blow-molding plastics, spray polyurethane foams, robotics, and such. For tools, I've looked how electric or air driven tools are easier on the body. If I can get uninteresting stuff purchased already fabricated, so much the better. No one gives a second thought to the fact that all artists buy ready-to-use paint rather than mixing up the paint from powders, but I think about this when I sometimes see artists who still use processes that have long been abandoned by commercial contractors and factories.

All of this is important at any age, and I've given ample examples in The Art World Dream, but as we become seniors, processes become more important. If I really were to analyze my development over the years, I can see that age (whether it's maturity, getting smarter or diminishing physical abilities) has had an influence as much as wanting to find a better operational method.

STUDIO HAZARDS

Artists often need extra health care after working for many years with hazardous materials within toxic working environments.   Artists never have the money for the safety equipment that large companies use. Which artist do you know who can afford $100,000 for the type of water-based fully enclosed exhaust system that a dealer's body shop uses for spray painting cars? There are medical emergency stations at all large manufacturers. I'm lucky to still have a $10 first-aid box in sight-- there's a lot more to do.

And over the years, I've had my hands and arms smothered with all kinds of paints, thinners, resins and who knows what. I've sprayed polyurethane foam, car lacquers and aerosol cans filled with fixative, paint, sealers and more. All of those have been absorbed through skin and nose. I've worked with sawdust, plaster dust, foam dust, metal dust, and of course, floor dust. You get the idea-- not the most antiseptic environment I could have chosen.

I've become a bit more selective in what I choose to have a bath in. I'm more conscientious of my environment, in the same way as I try, at least to a small extent, to use organic food and even to eat more vegetables and healthy alternatives. Like most, I succumb to my comfort foods, especially when eating out. My sloppiness in general living - and I must add that my lifestyle is way healthier compared to the average American who is overweight and under exercised - extends to my studio. I'm sure for those artists who have a near perfect eating and exercise routine at home, will extend that degree of discipline to their studio. But for most artists, habits can be improved.

This is not to preach, for I am a sinner too, but to make you aware that whatever shortcomings we have now, will only exacerbate our problems when we are older.

ART CAN BE HEAVY

I feel sorry for people in the book business-- it all seems so easy until you realize how heavy those boxes of books are-- which have to be moved into a store on a daily basis. Well, even if you "only" do painting, stretchers add up in weight, especially in the larger sizes. I never used to hesitate to move an 18-foot wide painting all by myself. I only had part-time interns and only part of the year, and rarely were they around when I really needed two minutes of help. It got even worse because I spent a good chunk of my life making sculptures. Fortunately, I was not into heavy metal sculptures but still, they all add up in weight. My joke was that even though a lot of my work was polyurethane foam or blow-molded plastics, 100 pounds of feathers is still a hundred pounds. A large volume of even light material adds up quickly. Even with help, I was involved in moving them about the studio, onto and off of trucks for exhibitions, and later moving them to more permanent storage spaces. Believe me, I try not to go near them today, except to supervise assistants-- my back and other body parts just won't take it.

Most Americans suffer from back pain to various degrees. Sitting at the computer with the wrong posture, men sitting with their stuffed wallets in one of their back pockets, lifting while bending over -- these are just a few of the bad habits that have led to chronic pain in such a large portion of the population. The process of making art is a physical chore and some of it can get pretty heavy. There's no magic alternative other than to hire help, and no one is cheap anymore. But I have become smarter about how often I need to move large works, and I've become smarter about lining up the help. There are compromises that we must make because other hands will never be as careful are your own hands-- and the more things are moved by non-experts, who are usually the sort of people available for employment by-the-hour, the more accidents will occur.

ART GETS BUSIER

As a much younger artist, I was into one basic style of painting. Then I started to do some prints, and experimented in other medias. My work later evolved more into sculptural constructions. Each year, my work went in additional directions. Some became huge projects, while I continued to experiment in all sorts of side ventures - small reliefs, models, paper collages and reliefs, etc. The point is, that after decades of working, my studio is no longer the simple one-product "factory" it once was. At any given moment, I have at least a dozen major projects involving different styles, methods and materials. I'll do blow-molded sculptures while I'll continue huge collaged paintings, while I continue a two-year, 250-foot storyboard, while I work on drawings and sketch plans for various large-scale installations, and so forth. Within my studio, I have at least ten mini-studios. Then I have areas for storage, woodworking, cleaning, spray-equipment, display, and so forth.

As my mind and body says to reduce and simplify and organize, instead each year my studio gets less manageable and more out of control. It's going in a contrary direction than I want.

What to do? There's no easy answer. Space helps, especially in my case. If I had to move things every time I wanted to undertake a new project, I'd have no time or energy left. Currently, at least all I have to do is walk a few feet to another of the mini-studio spaces.

I think most artists keep adding to their repertoire as they mature and develop, and at some point, there's so much going on, that it takes it's toll on the physical person.

I don't want to suggest that anyone ever reduce their workload, because opportunities are exciting; the more ideas and chances to realize your dreams, the better. You only have to be aware of the fact that an older artist can easily become overtaxed, and the result can be devastating. One needs a good support system in place to prevent disasters, and this will only happen if the artist is smart enough to think in advance about ways to prepare for work.

Economics

50 YEAR PLANNING VS 10 YEAR PLANNING

Financial advisors say that 30-year olds should start saving 10% to 15% of their salary towards retirement; this is a reasonable amount to set aside for the future. By the age of 40, in order to reach satisfactory retirement savings, 25% of their salaries need to be saved. If they wait until they are 50-years old, more than 50% of their salaries would have to go towards savings in order to save up enough for retirement. Obviously, if you wait until the 50s, it's going to be very difficult, probably too difficult, to achieve a satisfactory retirement income.

It is difficult for 30-year olds to take retirement seriously, unless they have a wife and children and are set in a career track where these goals are more on their minds, along with college savings for their children, along with insurance policies to protect their families in case of untimely death, and along with long-term mortgage payments. This is a responsible way to manage finances, but it's getting less common in today's difficult economic climate.

For artists, who have lower income on average and who have higher discretionary expenses because they want to create art that more often won't be sold or make a profit, retirement savings are less common. For artists, even with family to worry about, the strain of trying to do it all often works against the interests of long-term planning.

Financial planning sounds like a boring thing geared for conservative people. It also sounds like something that is only done by people who make so much income that they can afford to dabble in stocks and bonds. Yet the smart people, even those who are barely making it, use their brains to be smart about how to manipulate their lives to thrive with limited income.

That means thinking outside the box, living in non-traditional ways, and being 'street smart.' Studios are a priority for most artists in order to carry out work. Oddball properties can be a fraction of the cost of traditional houses or normal commercial/industrial spaces preferred by traditional people. Oddball commercial properties are often overlooked by traditional businesses. Artists can take advantage of these odd spaces because they don't need to achieve the same types of economic efficiencies that normal businesses have to worry about.

Finally, my emphasis is that what you can do over a 30 or 40 or 50-year period will be far more successful than those efforts squeezed into just a few years. It might not feel like much, doing a bit each year, but when you hit 50 or so, and discover how many assets you have at your disposal, you'll be smiling compared to the artists of comparable age barely getting by month to month.

I'll describe in detail later in the book, but I started my efforts in earnest in 1978. It is about 35 years later and I'm dealing with more than 160,000 square feet, of which more than half is for my personal use, while the rest supports the income. I never had much money; assets were accumulated little by little. We purchased our first house in 1974 for $34,000, in Washington DC. Commercial properties that I've purchased, beginning in 1978, had mortgages paid off, and with appreciation that increased just about every year, some were then sold and the proceeds reinvested into other properties. Thirty-five years later, those assets are finally helping me deal with my goals for the "other side" of my life - my so-called 'golden years.' And if I continue to be successful, it will preserve my work after I am gone.

Yes, it's no longer 1978, and in Washington D.C. and most cities, you can't buy a closet for those prices. But in other areas of the country, you can still get a house for $34,000 (or less) and you can still get good commercial space for similar amounts. Especially now, with a worldwide economic decline, there are ample opportunities. And when you purchase something, after you've considered all the issues that will be outlined in this book (and are mentioned in my other books), you will still benefit from gradual appreciation of a building, that over a period of years, if not decades, might be right smack in the middle of a booming neighborhood. The younger you start, the more you'll gain.

THE IRS FACTOR

I don't want this book to be a tax and legal primer on all kinds of federal and state laws. Suffice it to be stated that the government is not usually your friend. It will not allow you to deduct from your taxes more than the cost of materials if you donate a work to a museum, but if your friend donates that same work, your friend can deduct the full market value of the work. When you die, guess what? While you were alive you could only deduct the cost of materials, but suddenly, the IRS will value the work at "market value" in order to collect estate taxes, which your heirs will pay if your total estate runs above the maximum allowable for that year (keep tuned in; this amount changes from year to year, until Congress settles on a rate). So suddenly, your art might be valuable and your heirs might need to raise a lot of money to pay taxes. There are opportunities to get the valuation discounted, and higher valuations mean more taxes but it also means that once the art is inherited, the heir can donate the art and get a tax deduction for that assessed value. Museums would like Congress to change these laws but while there's been talk for decades and some attempts, the laws are not going favorably for the artists, nor for the museums that would be recipients of all the art that artists would like to donate to them for full tax deductions.

There are all sorts of ins and outs, and I highly recommend that you read <u>A Visual Artist's Guide to Estate Planning</u>, which was based on a conference and then published by the Marie Walsh Sharpe Art Foundation and the Judith Rothschild Foundation. They added a supplement in 2008 by attorney Barbara Hoffman that has many additional necessary details. There are many examples of artists' estates and artist foundations, many started or conceived while the artist was alive; in most cases, there were substantial assets and value in the art. Although I give an example later in the book, the main purpose of this book is to help the artist realize options; for the exact process, the artist will have to consult a lawyer and others who have the expertise in this area and for the laws of the state in which the artist is residing.

The idea that you don't have to be a household name to deal with estate planning, art foundations, establishing museums, and so forth, needs to be absorbed. The specifics are so numerous after one understands the basics, that I can only present the rudimentary concepts in this introduction. But do read further in their publication. There's not many other published resources out there geared for artists, although general estate planning books can of course be helpful.

INDEPENDENCE; HOW TO AVOID HAVING YOUR CHILDREN CARE FOR YOU

Rather than your children taking care of you, as was a more common practice a century ago, in today's strained economy, more and more children are living at home as adults and the parents are caring not only for them, but even for the grandchildren.

There will be conflicts about how your resources are used and to whom your assets will go upon death.

You will be concerned about your spouse, but don't expect your spouse, if you should predecease your spouse, to be able to administer your art estate. If you are lucky, he or she will join you in old age, and both of you will experience diminishing abilities.

At the same time, and forgive me if I sound negative, few children will want to deal with your desires or 'stuff.' They lead their own busy lives and have enough problems of their own. In most cases, I would not recommend that artists rely on their children to bail them out. The time commitment to take over hundreds or thousands of artworks, to deal with equipment and supplies and to deal with archiving, preserving and distributing your life's work upon your death, well, that's just more than most younger folks can take on. Even if you have a dealer or agent handling most of the work, it needs oversight.

So if you can't 'draft' or hire your children at super low rates, you'll have to ramp up your financial projections and find the funds to pay for someone who has the ability to do it right. You don't have to be rich; you simply have to plan far enough in advance so you'll have the funds when you need them.

GRANTS

The Adolph and Esther Gottlieb Foundation awards up to $10,000 for mature artists, and they have assistance grants for mature artists mostly who have special and emergency needs. But grants aimed at senior artists are rare. Grants can always be applied for, but I never expect them. As we get older, I think being awarded grants gets even harder. Maybe you'll have better luck than I have had; and the same goes for public commissions. Committees comprised of architects and city planners rarely go after groundbreaking art; they want public art that will please the public-- something safe. Big-name artists have had better luck solely due to reputation, but for those of us a level or two below, it's a tricky path to navigate unless you really have spent your career building up the record that the grantors demand to see before giving you the commission.

If you decide to set up your own unique space to show your work, there might be small grants available, if you spend the time to apply. Don't overlook arts grants aimed at regional or local efforts. Such a space, that is open to the public and which you can claim might be an attraction and be a tourist or an educational asset to the area, might be a winning candidate. It will give you some support but I would not look to grants for other than possible bonus money.

LEGAL ISSUES

WILLS AND STUFF

There are ample advice books and articles that you can read about estate planning, wills, and principles of trusts. You'll quickly understand not only the fundamentals of these end-of-life issues, but you'll quickly learn how your assets should be in a revocable trust and be part of your will. The essence of this legal step is that, upon your death, your assets can be distributed in the way you wish them to be, without the estate going into probate, which basically means a judge will decide what's what. Probate can take months and months to get through and in the end, decisions are made that perhaps you did not intend, and expenses will go much higher. A trust is simple, direct and to the point.

Most good books will cover all kinds of issues- protecting minor children, children with special needs, divorce, non-martial property, determining how to add up your assets, state differences, pensions, survivor benefits, passing down businesses to heirs, and the list goes on and on. But really, if you are at all inspired by the end of this book, do go out and get a basic primer on financial planning, estates, trusts and financial issues related to retirement. Somewhere you'll fit within these categories, and you'll also see that you are different from most. After all, you are an artist, and you want to protect your life's work.

But in addition to this, if you are following advice about planning more carefully about the distribution and/or continuation of your art in some form, then you will need to do additional legal work.

I will tell you that you'll save a fortune by reading a couple of books first, making an outline of your plans and then, and only then, talk to an attorney or expert. The outline alone will put some cold water to some of your notions.

You might value your art very highly in monetary terms, but the reality is that your art is more likely a liability. It probably can't be sold quickly, if at all, if it's not selling regularly while you are alive. A sale once in a while when you have a gallery show is not what most would refer to as a "robust market" for your work. Unfortunately, with your art come demands - to pay for storage space and related staff and utilities, to pay for someone to inventory your art, to preserve your art, to handle your art for potential sale or distribution, to wrap and ship your art, to insure your art, to pay for administration and accounting services, to pay for taxes or at least to file returns if none are due, and to eventually figure out a plan for what to do because the chances are that either there will be art left over that can't be sold, or that the process will continue for a very long time.

With this potential liability comes a responsibility to figure out the game plan. The more art your have and the more you value your art, the more urgent it is to finalize a plan.

The most obvious structure is to form a foundation. A foundation can take many forms, and it can have a limited or unlimited lifespan, depending on your assets. But it is a legal entity that, in theory, can own your art and real estate and other assets, and can carry out your wishes.

Obviously, the foundation need not own all your assets, as you might want to provide for family and other causes. But it seems like the structure most suitable, especially as applies to taxes.

By the way, most people think of the main art objects as what needs to be preserved, but don't forget the many archival papers as well as copyrights. Intellectual property issues are getting more and more complicated as the Internet spreads knowledge all over the globe at lightning speed.

ESTATE TAXES

I'm not a lawyer and I won't pretend to give you legal advice. Estate taxes can be a big deal, but more often for those with a big enough name with art valued in the millions.

A lawyer I used to know had a famous judgment in his favor when he argued that when art is disposed of upon an artist's death, the fact that so much of it has to be sold versus selling it a little at a time over many years, creates a depression in the market value and thus he was able to get the IRS to substantially discount its assessment of the David Smith estate.

Even if you have sold periodically, your market value might be so low that you can report to the IRS a value that won't be taxable. However, depending on your sales record, this can be a dicey matter; better review this with your accountant first.

Taxes on your art can be avoided completely if you donate your art to a charitable organization. If your art is highly in demand, museums (major as well as those connected to universities) might want to take your art, and you can make your art a gift, to be legally transferred upon your death. However, almost all museums will, at best, accept one work. The expense to store a work in their collection is much higher than your cost to store the same work in your studio.

If your art is not in demand and no museum is interested, then you can find another charitable organization to take it. Those not in the business of art will look at your art as a possible asset to sell in order to raise cash. This is not in your best interest.

Ideally, you want your art to be preserved and shown to future generations. That means you need a specific type of organization. And the charitable organization can be, and should be, the foundation that you set up to receive your art either before or upon your death. This prevents the government from coming in and taxing the value, since it has all been donated, and you are free to use those assets as per your plans to preserve, exhibit and promote your art.

Obviously, the principles here apply for all your taxable assets, and so stocks, bonds, cash and other material things you own should all be considered in the mix.

I can't tell you enough that tax laws differ from state to state, and even federal laws will affect artists differently depending on individual circumstances. Consult a tax and/or estate attorney and/or certified public accountant, and get your plan merged into a legal structure that will actually work for your benefit.

Foundations - The Key

FOUNDATIONS

Foundations can be established to put your art into a trust, to be run by trustees whom you pick (initially) to carry out your wishes. Operating foundations can be in the form of a museum, for example, that will operate to show your art. Other foundations contribute assets in the form of grants, and the smaller ones often have limited time spans, so that at some point, the money is spent and the foundation closes.

Although operating foundations can be set up to use up assets at some point in the future, so for example, a thirty-year run might be a satisfactory outcome, I'm more interested in the operating foundation that will exist into the indefinite future. Such a foundation usually has substantial wealth to begin with; trying to do this on a limited allowance will take some 'thinking outside the box.' While challenging, it is possible.

Most experts would advise you to have at least two million dollars to carry out some sort of program. Administrative fees alone, legal and accounting, can cost the foundation $10,000 to $25,000 a year. Then one must hire someone to manage the foundation and all the parts. That salary, plus office, storage, exhibition related expenses, archival costs, etc, all add up to a pretty penny. That is why that even a couple of million dollars can be used up in a relatively short time.

But if you think in terms of cheaper real estate, and doing just a limited number of activities, you can stretch the dollar much further.

Foundations, as mentioned elsewhere, can be complicated and involve resolving issues with family, executors, tax assessors, and so forth. However, the fairly straightforward ones are substantial enough to stand on their own.

In order to be accepted as a 501c3 charitable organization, a foundation must be organized as an educational facility. However, the mission statement of an artist's foundation, to manage the artist's estate, will most likely state that the purpose is to make the art available to the public and to educate the public about the artist's work and process. In other words, what you want to do is preserve and exhibit the art, and that is an educational endeavor, acceptable to the government.

Example of Mission Statement used in an application as part of articles of organization: (see sample by-laws and full articles of organization statement at the end of the book)

A. TO PROMOTE AND CARRY OUT ALL CHARITABLE AND EDUCATIONAL PURPOSES WITHIN THE MEANING OF SECTION 501(C)(3) OF THE INTERNAL REVENUE CODE OF 1986, AS AMENDED (OR ANY SUCCESSOR PROVISIONS THEREFOR), INCLUDING, BUT NOT LIMITED TO THE PURPOSES MORE PARTICULARLY DESCRIBED BELOW: TO PROMOTE, CONSERVE, PRESERVE AND EXHIBIT THE SCULPTURES/PAINTINGS AND PIECES OF ART OF _____name of artist_____ FOR THE BENEFIT OF THE PUBLIC; TO EXHIBIT HIS/ HER VISUAL ART, AND TO ORGANIZE PERFORMANCES OF HIS WRITTEN AND DESCRIBED WORKS; TO COLLECT, CONSERVE, PRESERVE AND EXHIBIT, ON A TEMPORARY OR PERMANENT BASIS, THE ORIGINAL WORKS OF OTHER ARTISTS AS SUCH WORKS RELATE TO THE WORKS OF _____name of artist_____ AND IN THE CONTEXT OF SUCH RELATIONSHIPS; TO ORGANIZE AND SPONSOR EDUCATIONAL ACTIVITIES RELATED TO HIS/HER ART INCLUDING, BUT NOT LIMITED TO SEMINARS, WORKSHOPS AND PERFORMANCES; TO PROMOTE, SUPPORT, FOSTER AND/ OR CONTRIBUTE TO THE ESTABLISHMENT, MAINTENANCE AND OPERATION OF A MUSEUM FOR THE PUBLIC EXHIBITION OF _____name of artist's_____ ART.

One must be very careful to keep it all transparent, and to make sure there are no conflicts of interest, where trustees are using the foundation for personal gain. Keep it straight, and you won't have anyone doubting your mission.

YOU DON'T HAVE TO BE RICH TO HAVE A FOUNDATION

A lawyer can set up a non-profit corporation and apply for 501c3 status (which means the organization is approved by the U.S government as a charitable organization and people who donate money to it can deduct those donations from their taxes) for a couple of thousand dollars. If you are really smart or desperate, you could probably do it yourself. Organizational papers are public records; get a copy of a similar organization, copy them and change details as appropriate, and apply. The annual fees can be zero to a few hundred dollars, depending on the state in which you are residing.

Once you say you have a foundation, people will think you're rich! But you'll know what the truth is. You'll have to be very careful going forward and dot all the "i's."

Of course, it doesn't pay to have a foundation unless you have a use for it. And if you do have a use for it, you'll need to think very carefully of the consequences.

For example, if a 501c3 charitable organization owns property, and the property is used for the charitable purposes, then usually that entity will not have to pay real estate taxes (if the property is being used for charitable purposes). That's a big saving.

It is also a way to consider putting your art into a legal structure in order to protect it from being sold or distributed contrary to your wishes. Keep in mind, that your donation of art to a charitable foundation is not tax deductible except to the extent of the cost of materials. So if you donate/give a painting valued at $10,000, you can only deduct most likely a hundred dollars for the cost of the paint and canvas. If you had sold that same painting to someone for $1,000, and over the ensuing years it appreciated, and that owner then donated the painting to the same charitable organization, that person could deduct the full $10,000 from his or her taxes. There are other issues, but that's the main principle.

Alternatively to a regular sale, it is possible to "sell" your works for one-time use only, perhaps at a discount, so that the art is promised not be resold at some future point but instead donated to such a charitable organization (almost like renting your art for a specified period), but that would take careful early planning. And it would not help you, the artist, except that the work might come back into an artist-founded museum collection.

A CALL FOR DONORS

All charitable organizations, all theaters and all art museums ask for money. They seek money though memberships, through various donor categories, and through a variety of fundraising efforts. Most museums only pay a third to less than a half of their expenses through attendance income. The rest comes from grants, endowments, and donations.

You are looking ahead. It would be (unless you have something I can't imagine) almost impossible to get sizable donations outside of family to your proposed art foundation and/or museum. People give to established museums. But you really don't want money now, necessarily. You want money when all your plans kick into gear, upon your death. So you might know of friends, collectors or supporters who have money and may have fewer family members to whom they will bequeath their assets. Would they contribute some money to your proposed museum upon their death? Giving money away after you are gone is often an easier thought than having one's money depart while one is alive.

Now you are competing with any just cause-- not just other art museums, but for any need. Your prospects might feel that helping the hungry, under-educated, those with medical challenges - are far more worthy than supporting your tiny art museum. And that's a tough one to debate.

However, the smaller the charitable organization, the easier it is to make an impact. A hundred thousand dollar gift to a major art museum will receive a nice thank you, perhaps even a few invitations for dinners, but it won't make much of a dent in their overall operation. The same sized gift to a small organization, in this case to your enterprise, is enough for you to offer to "name a room" after that donor. You get the idea; donors like to see that their gift will do something dramatic, and that's your main argument. Perhaps this potential donor has had an influence upon your career; that's a connection that you can use -- to acknowledge that prospective donor's special relationship to the proposed museum in a special way - perhaps with a plaque, or naming of a gallery, or in some other way.

WHOM DO YOU CHOOSE?

Obviously, whoever is going to deal with your art after you are gone, should be on the young side. Your children can do a wonderful job with oversight as long as they are not burdened with the actual work. They might have the incentive and love to see that it's done right, and you most probably will give some of the art to your children. Your children also have intimate knowledge about the work and can give invaluable advice.

The spouse is normally the person with the initial burden by default, although usually the age is too close to the artist's age to oversee a project that might take decades, unless the artist has an untimely early death. After younger family members, who as I indicated earlier are too busy to take on the task, gallery dealers are often selected. However, age is a matter for dealers as well, and because they are in a fickle business, not all galleries will survive. Plus, of course, as I've been saying repeatedly, most serious artists just don't have the market strength to make it worthwhile to a dealer who really sees art as potential profit.

Lawyers, accountants and financial advisors are usually the next logical choices, but again, most of them have limited knowledge about art and they are expensive - these are folks who are used to hourly billing. In this group, a young associate whom you think might be at the firm for a decade or two after you die is a better choice, so hopefully he or she can take on the work even if he or she leaves the firm, or if the firm doesn't survive for some reason.

A few foundations have filled the trustee posts with artists, the idea being that only artists can understand really what was the artist's intent on preserving the art, or what really matters in the art world in the case of a foundation that is using the funds to help outside art causes. Nothing is foolproof. There are well-publicized cases in the art world where artist-trustees sided with gallery dealer-trustees because they wanted to be given shows themselves. There are always splits and self-gaining motives involved, and few boards maintain 100% purity. The more money that's involved, the more temptation there is for corruption.

Bottom line? It's not easy. Setting up a trust and foundation, getting board members to serve, and figuring out who will have to be the main paid person-- these are the decisions that have to be made carefully and in consultation with whomever you are considering.

Finally, please include in your deliberations the idea that you, the artist, can have a major role if you start the foundation while you are alive. It is a way to ease into the system and fix the flaws. Of course, this can put you at odds with how you allocate your time. You don't want to drown in legal and business issues. But this process can also serve as an opportunity to realize new work, as you will read when I talk about my current project.

When to Activate Your Plans

IF YOU ARE LUCKY TO BE IN YOUR 20S OR 30S

I know that this book will attract readers who are close to or well within the AARP market. However, if you are lucky enough to be in your 20s or 30s and reading this, you will benefit much.

I was that age when I began thinking about permanent exhibition space for my work. For most of my early career, I had studios for a year or two before moving on. Usually I had to move because either I out-grew the space or the initial low-rent was no longer available.

Later on, if I had a studio for five years, I counted myself fortunate. One of my great studios was a 5,000 square foot (later expanded to 6,000) studio on one of the main avenues in Washington D.C., across from the Washington Hilton, just a few blocks from all the art galleries and three blocks from our townhouse. I could walk to the studio, and go home for dinner and to help with the kids, and then have an easy walk back to do some evening work. The space had been a restaurant in an old apartment building that had a fire and was abandoned. When I saw the discarded space, it needed a lot of work, including filling in trenches with concrete. With exposed pipes, the bare-bones space was perfect for studio work, with double doors leading to the lobby and street. It's hard to talk about what money was worth 40 years ago, but believe me when I say that $150 per month for the space that included heat and electricity was an incredibly low rate even at that time.

Any studio where I could stay for five years was a success, and I had more - a total of eight years before the building was sold and converted into a condominium. Then I was out searching again, with pressure to keep making art and meeting my exhibition commitments. Not to repeat a story that you can read about in detail in my other books, I found an incredible deal in a not-so-great neighborhood - a 34,000 square foot four-story warehouse for a bargain (I'm using that word a lot but that's what I've needed in order to make my plans work within my budget) price of $66,000 with seller financing. That was 1978. I ended up using 14,000 square feet of the space for my personal studio, as I eventually renovated and rented out the remaining space to pay for all my operating expenses.

However, believe it or not, after too short of a time, my studio filled up. At the same time, I had dreams of creating large installations that would be very involved and needed lots more space. These were not projects where I could just set up in a few weeks. These were expansive undertakings and I needed space and money and time to do them well. Where to do that? I had no more room in my studio.

I also began to wonder if anyone might financially sponsor my installations. As I've mentioned, the grass looks greener for artists of small works when I think how hard it is for installation artists. To assemble such a large work, usually if the artist is lucky to have respectable exhibition space, it will be for a 6 to 8 week run, and then the materials have to be disassembled and stored in boxes. Usually the artist takes lots of photographs as a way to document the work, and with the realistic expectation that the work probably will never be seen again.

Think about all the expense it takes for a museum to accept and store a painting in their collection and you'll sympathize when they don't accept large installation pieces in their collection.

When an artist-turned-curator wanted to mount a show from the SFMoMA collection three years ago and preliminarily selected my large relief, he and assistants had to make arrangements to see the actual work, which was in a crate in the museum's storage facility across the city. The staff there had to get the crate out and open it up. Not an easy thing to do just to peek at one work that was at least in one piece. Imagine if that curator wanted to consider including an installation piece that was in many pieces - just the storage alone would deter the museum from accepting that work (unless it was made by a super-star name of course). So installation artists, sculptors, multi-media artists- all have a rougher time in many ways than those who create their art within reasonable dimensions.

So thinking all about this, and how hard it would be to get a museum to sponsor my proposed installations, I started to wonder whether I could control everything from start to finish, including the initial installation and perhaps a permanent exhibition operation, rather than going through all the work for a few weeks and then taking it all down.

I also started to think about the attraction my work might have. Different artwork attracts different audiences. For example, realism and figurative art has a larger viewing market than abstraction. My robotic sculptures seem to mesmerize whoever walks by. Often how the work is displayed can also expand a market. Museums aim to explain art to a larger and perhaps less knowledgeable audience. Public art that is outside is much easier to access than art inside a museum that charges admission. Art that is around the walls of a restaurant is seen because people are eating, whereas the same art might draw a smaller audience in an art gallery. Art that is good can also be fun to a lay audience, depending on the images, or if it has interactive features, and so forth.

Certain periods of my art have been more popular to a lay audience than others. For example, when I included three-dimensional illusion in early abstract wall constructions, I noticed how lay people (usually workmen who were in the studio for another reason) were drawn to the work much more easily than my more conceptual or abstract pieces without illusion. I don't do art that is popular; I make my art and then I observe that some styles/periods are more popular than others. I stick to my standards, whether it's liked and popular or not.

And so, as I started to think about doing large installations, I thought that perhaps I could have a place that could also be open to the public and perhaps I could figure out ways to attract an audience. In other words, I needed experimental space and rather than it be shut away in a back part of town or out in the boon docks, I wondered if I couldn't find a place that was more accessible.

If I had an accessible place, could I display some of my work so the public could see whatever I might want to show it off? If I could do that, and since some of my processes were involving theme-park technologies, I naturally started to think about Disney and how he had taken his comic art ideas and built an environment to show them off in such a way that millions of people travel to his parks each year. Could I do something like this on a miniature level? Could I create a cultural theme park ride and a mini-park?

When I used to drive outside of Washington, I spotted rural commercial properties on ample land that were no longer in business and wondered if I could convert them to a live/work studio and public space. When I traveled, I spotted ample vacant land and buildings in towns all across the nation, and each time, I thought about whether I could add a second destination to my life.

Much of this has to do with controlling my destiny - who chooses my work for inclusion in a show or collection, how the public can access my work, and so forth. While I've been fortunate to be selected for numerous exhibitions and to be in museum collections, those successes only affect a small fraction of my artistic output.

Most of my work gets created and stays forever in my studio, and the public never gets to see the work.

So as we think about what happens after death to our art, there's a direct correlation to how we think about exhibition during our active lifetime. Although I didn't think about after-death issues that much at the time, I did think of permanence and about how an exhibition space could economically operate in a break-even manner. It was at this age period that I researched and explored options that I couldn't immediately put to use.

An aggressive plan to put your art on display during your active years could have bearing on how it might continue upon your death. Plans that are proposed to you in this book must be initiated during your lifetime. The larger question is whether these efforts can be expanded to cover your art and your dreams after you are no longer active.

Finally, a word to those in your 20s and 30s. Be respectful of older artists. It's fine to try to change the direction of art in new ways, but remember who planted your roots. I'll never forget when I ran the Contemporary Artists Center; we used to invite some of the biggest artist and museum director names in the country. One time, Grace Hartigan came for a few days and talked after one of our dinners. Some of the younger artists-in-residence got impatient and left, even though she was talking about when she "used to go to Jackson's studio." I admonished them afterwards by telling them that when she goes, all that they'll know about Jackson Pollack will be from third-hand sources. Here was someone who was relating to them art history in the first-person! It was a missed opportunity for them. She is no longer alive and that link is gone forever.

I've had conversations with some big names in the art world - Rauschenberg, Warhol, Newman - and I always appreciated the chance to talk and learn. It was never about whether I wanted to imitate them-- my art was in a different direction by then anyway, but I showed my respect for the ones who made or were making art history.

So now I'm in the older league and I see the younger "kids" who think they are so smart they need not bother to talk to their predecessors. *That's their mistake.*

IF YOU ARE IN YOUR 40S - THE IDEAL AGE

When you've reached the age of 40, you are at your prime! You have your full strength, with two decades of experience. You have a body of work to worry about and hopefully you'll be near to having your maximum exposure (fame) to the public and to having your highest sales. And you will have matured to the point where, if you haven't already, you can have a realistic glimpse of being age 50 or 60, and so you'll take traditional retirement planning ads more seriously.

In addition, you will still be open for change; I was near this age when I made the most dramatic change of my life, giving up years of experience in Washington D.C., with shows, connections and a huge studio, to go to what I then regarded as "no man's land" in order to work unobstructed in gigantic studio space several times the size of my Washington studio. It was also the time when I decided not to continue with the traditional gallery route, and take an adventurous independent path in life. The move required renovating a huge mill, it required packing and moving - and I might add that it required seven full-sized moving vans -- and then setting up shop again to do creative work. I might not have taken this on a decade later, and I might not have appreciated the opportunity a decade earlier.

This is the time when you can take ideas presented in this book and put them to best use, because you'll have time to work towards your goals gradually. You might easily have twenty years to carry out dramatic projects and have the supporting environment to preserve them.

This is also the age when you get a bit more realistic about your dreams-- not to lessen what you want, but to understand that the likelihood that you'll be picked among hundreds of thousands of artists and made a superstar is slim, but that you can still attain your creative freedom by pursuing and controlling your own destiny. Read on.

50S AND 60S - THERE'S STILL TIME

You still have a couple, maybe three or even four, of decades to work. So you have time. But your strength might be decreasing some, and if you haven't done much to prepare for your 'end game,' then start to worry and decide to rectify the situation immediately. There's still enough time if you begin to follow a definite plan.

This is the age when retirement from whatever 'day' job you have is within sight, and your income will shift soon with social security, pension, Medicare, and so forth. It is perhaps the best time to decide about how you want to live once your need to be in a particular place has ended. Usually a job or young family keeps you pinned down. With kids in college and with 'day' job retirement approaching, you are free to examine exactly where you would ideally like to live and locate your studio.

So with more freedom than colleagues who are a decade or two younger, if you are mentally open to new ideas, you can do a lot. You'll have to execute your plans with more care than someone younger, just because your physical strength might not be what it once was. You also have less time to correct mistakes, so you'll need to be pretty sure of your moves.

I will tell you that I know several people who, in my opinion, have the energy of artists half their age. Why is that? I think it's because they never get so trapped by a route that they miss jumping at a new opportunity that can spring from anywhere least expected.

So if you think that it's too late for you, then you'll have to make some adjustments in the way you analyze your work and place in life. At 80, maybe you can make an argument against drastic change, but if you haven't yet collected social security, you should feel free.

IF YOU ARE IN THE PANIC YEARS

What can I say? I'll not blame you because no one wrote a book like this for you to read twenty or more years ago. So perhaps you didn't think about these ideas. Is it too late? Maybe, but maybe not. If by good luck or chance or hard work you've made some money or have a studio space fully paid for, you can still put these assets to good use.

But realize that at this age, you will need to do something pretty quickly if you want to avoid having your work destroyed by neglect after you are gone.

An interesting study about older artists was called "Above Ground" - Information about Artists III; Special Study Focus New York City Aging Artists." You can read the full study at http://www.tc.columbia.edu/centers/rcac/pdf/IOA_III_Aging_FULL_REPORT_Final.pdf. Compiled by Research Center for Arts and Culture, the study was funded by the Pollock-Krasner Foundation and the Cornell Institute for Translational Research on Aging. Although the study zeros in on NYC artists, many of the statistics are probably shared by artists around the country.

Among the statistics presented in the study, 61% of artists have made no preparations for their artwork after their death, only 10% have made plans to donate their work to an institution, and 17.1% plan to leave work to their heirs. As the study notes, there is no certainty that the heirs or institutions want the work or will know what to do with the work. When asked about a formal estate plan, 97.1% responded that they have no plan whatsoever. Nationally, 44% of Americans at least have wills, but for artists, the rate is only 22.9%.

By the way, 94.1% report that they have no studio assistants, so the archival work that has to be carried out will probably not be done. Several artists did indicate a desire for an organization to assist artists with archival related work. Although the Joan Mitchell Foundation has helped a few artists with archival work, for the vast majority of artists, that's just wishful thinking. From the few depressing quotes, it seems that many artists only finally realize the problem when they observe what happens to the art of a colleague who died. Most artists worry more about keeping up with studio rent and not being evicted, and some simply discard older work in order to keep their art inventory down. For those who barely can pay the monthly rent and are well into their 70s or 80s, I don't have magic answers. But some artists are more fortunate, and those are the ones who should set an example.

If you are older, you are smarter. If you are smarter, then you know how to organize the issues. Make a list. Write down all your art assets, your operational needs, your space needs, your future plans and see if all of these components can be reshuffled. Pretend that you are a consultant and look at your lists as if you were the advisor to another artist. Usually it's far easier to give advice to someone else than to give yourself advice-- or to take the advice.

One thing that you do need to do is face reality. Your time is more limited than someone younger. You should be current with all your assets, wills, estate planning, etc. You need to really inventory your studio, including all your art, and figure out the end game. You need to be realistic not only about what you can accomplish in a short time, but also realistic about the value or demand for your art. Then you'll have to make some hard decisions.

If you have the resources, then none of the ideas that are mentioned in this book are necessarily out of your reach. To fulfill those goals, you'll have to increase the funding that otherwise can be done gradually over time. There's no reason why you can't find space, line up trustees and managers to execute your plan and carry it all out. It just won't be quite as easy unless you have the ability to finance your plans.

Finally, analyze your current situation. Make sure you are getting optimal use out of your time, out of your studio, and out of your assets and resources. If not, make adjustments. You should have a pretty clear view of what you want to accomplish in your 'end game.' If you are not creating what historians will call your "late masterpieces," then figure out what you need to do in order to make them.

The Government and More

GOVERNMENTAL ROLE?

In a Canadian census study, senior artists made about 40% of what the average Canadian worker of comparable age made. In other words, artists seem to be in real trouble when they get older (as reported by the Hill Strategies Research study). Their study also compared services to artists in other countries. For example, in Austria, if art income drops below a certain level, artists receive an increase in government support through a pension supplement. All I can say is - don't hold your breath that the U.S. government will increase social security payments to artists, under any circumstances.

Programs for artists in more socialistic European countries vary from basic support plans for all people in the arts based on income, to support for mature artists based on merit - i.e. you need to be recognized. But some European countries are in so much financial trouble that they are underfinanced and can give no support. Nevertheless, basic services are generally more liberal in many European countries than in the United States, especially for medical care. In at least one case, Norway, there is a special 5% fee paid when purchasing art that goes for a fund to help artists. Realistically, I would not hope for such foresight in the U.S., where the National Endowment for the Arts no longer gives grants to individual artists and where too many political candidates advocate for the removal of all support for the arts.

The National Endowment for the Arts got a bit into art and aging, but really only because studies have shown that creative activity is good for seniors (you can look up the National Center for Creative Aging). Programs that they support seem to support exposing seniors to art, not especially aiming benefits for established senior artists. I'm not concerned in this book with turning seniors into artists or using art for therapy. Rather, I want to find more support for serious artists as they become seniors.

However, it's not a total loss in the U.S.; there are a handful of guilds for actors, musicians and writers that have pension plans for members, as well as some housing alternatives. Partners for Livable Communities is one organization that has dealt with aspects of the arts as it impacts communities. There is much more to do. We'll discuss artist communities later in the book.

Among private attempts, the Artist Pension Trust was first started in New York but has since expanded to several world capitals. The essence of the program is to receive works each year from accepted artists (two per year for five years, then one per year for the next five years, then one work every two years thereafter, for a total of 20 works) and to try to promote and sell these works, while using the funds to guarantee the artists a steady income. The idea of pooling 250 artists is that some will do better than others, supporting the weaker ones. It's an imaginative first step, but only affects a fraction of the artists needing such support. Plus, according to their web site, the selection team is headed up by David Ross (former director of the Whitney and SFMoMA), which brings in the same selection system as is currently in the art world, keeping away those already outside the mainstream. My guess is that the accepted artists are already doing better financially than the average artist.

In many ways, this Artist Pension Trust is similar to the investment idea I described in my book, The Art World Dream, and which I'll mention again as a potential business. In the case of the Artist Pension Trust, it is based on being accepted; in the hypothetical example I described, artists could 'buy ' into the system for similar benefits. In reality, with the various alternatives that I describe in this book, an artist can go about setting something up individually, or going in collectively with a few other artists. It is also possible to enlarge this concept to include general membership from a greater number of participants.

My focus is not to add a small step for solving a national problem, but to offer specific and far-reaching strategies that one artist (or perhaps a few collectively), without being beholden to any funder or government agency, can initiate successfully on his or her own. There are many options available. Read on and then decide if any of them are right for you.

SERVICES FOR SENIOR ARTISTS

There are many types of services that agencies could initiate to help people in the arts. Someone should start an AARP for artists. Senior artists should get special discounts from the art supply stores, they should get special treatment from art museums, they should have special lobbyists who can promote their interests before Congress, to the National Endowment for the Arts, and before other national interest groups.

Despite the fact that one study indicated that one in ten Americans are active in the arts (play in a band, sing in a choir, paint in their basement studio, etc), I've never heard a question asked in a major Presidential debate about the arts. In fact, most candidates fear talking about funding the arts because censorship and government money given for scandalous art have made this a volatile subject in the past.

Seniors really don't get much respect. The kids get all the attention-- apparently they have most of the disposable money to spend on whatever companies are selling. Senior discounts really don't equal the regular discounts you can get online.

OK, once in a while we save a dollar or two in a museum admission, but I think museums should be free to artists; after all, without artists, the museums wouldn't be in business.

Nevertheless, as we begin to focus on this area, perhaps we'll start to catch up with our European counterparts. There are ways to perhaps influence regional and state arts councils more than the national government. I am a big believer that more artists should spend just a little time in working for the betterment of their colleagues. A letter, a telephone call, even an email can make a difference if many participate.

GOVERNMENTAL SOLUTIONS

A small cultural venue financed by a single artist would be more feasible in a smaller community rather than in New York City, but of course, local support for your venture would be essential. You want this art idea of yours to be well received, for people to recommend it to their friends and family, for people to support it in other ways, including donation of money and time, and if it's a success, it will impact positively not only for your art but upon your neighbors, upon other artists considering such a project, and upon the community at large.

Even in larger cities, circles of friends and colleagues can help. Certainly joint marketing can save costs and support similar art spaces. Museums might be able to hold your hand in ways that might not be apparent, although I've found that the entire world, from small organizations to giant ones, seem so worried about their own camp, they have little time to help the little guys.

I mention this quickly because there are structural solutions that the National Endowment for the Arts could initiate. Because of scandals, they no longer fund individual artists. Even support for individual exhibitions is down-- God forbid that one of the art pieces should offend an important member of Congress.

My solution for governmental grants is simple - have every large grant application by a major museum (and these amounts often go into the $100,000 range) include helping a smaller arts organization in their geographical area - to the extent of 10%. So in the $100,000 example, $10,000 would go to a smaller organization (or groups) and the museum would have to select and then oversee the participation of the smaller organization. The idea is to force big museums to be kinder to their up and coming smaller alternative art spaces or non-profit arts groups. At the same time, there would be no more burden on the government, because it would all be part of the same application process. With a stroke of a pen by the National Endowment for the Arts, hundreds and perhaps thousands of small arts groups would have critical- even life saving - help. Keep this in mind as you read about the artist-museums that I advocate in the subsequent sections of the book.

The Real Foundation: Studio Real Estate

STUDIO STRATEGIES

Art making is a physical activity. It involves many processes, and although there are a lot of conceptual artists around, the bulk of art is still a physical object. This object is fabricated in a studio. For that reason alone, the studio becomes the heart of the fabrication process. As work expands, the studio takes on more and more functions.

Artists have basic things in common when dealing with studio space. It's either rented (or gifted for the artist's use) or owned; it's either part of residential premises or it's commercial/industrial. And it's either in a neighborhood that might be acceptable for public viewing/visitors or it's not.

Within the studio, artists do a variety of processes. But generally, almost all artists have actual working space, some office type space for computer/paper work, some storage space for materials, some storage space for completed or ongoing work, and perhaps other types of space for display or specialized processes and needs. Somewhere there might be bathroom, kitchenette and relaxing space.

That's a basic studio. There are too many artists who cram all this into a single room, and there are many who run professional operations that more resemble a typical small manufacturer than the "romantic artist painting away at an easel in an atelier in front of a massive window or under a skylight. "

Ample studio space affords the artist opportunities to expand the work. Ample space allows for more experimentation with a variety of attempts, as several projects can be worked on simultaneously. As the artist ages, the studio becomes the workhorse. It takes the abuse and displays the triumphs. And in our senior years, it allows the work to be assembled and archived. My emphasis will be to determine two main things: Will the studio be workable for the older artist, and will it allow for options when the artist is no longer around?

REAL ESTATE - STUDIO OPTIONS

Even if you were not thinking about your senior years, early on you should have (and maybe it's not too late) have thought about purchasing your studio rather than renting it. Rents continue to climb; eventually it could put the space out of your financial reach. Only those few artists who sell continuously can justify renting and letting the landlord have all the maintenance headaches.

If you purchase your studio space, in theory, you can pay off your mortgage after a number of years, and by owning it free and clear, you can use it without debt service or sell it for a profit. That's the idea if all goes well.

There have been plenty of artists who took some risk and purchased studio space before an area was trendy, and made off like bandits. In later years, the profits come in handy because it can be traded to increase income, or to trade for larger quarters, as well as to have some security in older age.

I've emphasized this in both my books, and The Art Studio/Loft Manual deals exclusively about real estate issues. For me, real estate is as essential to master and be successful in as it is to stretch and prime a new canvas if you are a painter, or to build an armature if you're a sculptor. Space enables you to carry out your work. The smarter you are about that, the more you can potentially do. I won't repeat myself now, except that as we talk about the senior years, how you have approached your studio space becomes critical. You'll read later about some examples of successful real estate purchases, where the properties are now in transition, fulfilling the goal of preserving art after the artists are gone.

If you are still a few years away from social security, it's not too late to reexamine your options. And if you are going to reevaluate your space needs, in addition to materials and work already completed, you might also think about your future work -- not only about your working requirements, but also about what will happen to your work after that.

One theme that will be repeated is whether your studio can do double duty. Can it be a place to create art, and then later, can it be a place to show your art after you are gone? Can the public access your space easily, including those with disabilities, or is it a third floor walkup down an alley?

If you own the space, and if the space is accessible, and if there's potential for studio as well as retail or public use, then the options for you open up considerably. If you are considering new studio quarters, then these issues should be considered in your search.

THE BURDENS

I don't want to whitewash the issues regarding real estate in general, and studios specifically. Purchasing and maintaining studio space can sap your energy and use up your resources. There are many precautions, from zoning issues to major structural defects to hazardous waste pitfalls - and the list goes on. Many are outlined in <u>The Art Studio/Loft Manual</u> but I need to touch upon them again.

It's a bit like building stretchers. If you have the money, you can contract the work out. You can also hire people do it in your studio. Most artists, however, got their hands dirty in building and stretching and priming their own canvases.

Similarly, most artists are very hands-on about their studio spaces. Even for those who rent, the build-out of a studio to customize the space for an individual fabrication process can be very involved.

Ownership of a studio space often expands the issues that an artist has to worry about. But properly managed, with a smart purchase price in an appreciating neighborhood, the long-term rewards far outweigh the work that goes into it.

Admittedly, I'm an extreme example as to the amount of space that one can own. It is a business onto itself, and one that few artists would want to take on in addition to concentrating on their art. Personally, I find it a necessary chore that allows me so much freedom to create, that I put up with it all. Other artists have their day jobs- like teaching for example. A sculptor I know who has had many commissions spends equal amounts of time dealing with developers and engineers and architects. Life for an artist is full of work that's not very creative, but all part of keeping up the infrastructure so that art can be made.

Because I feel that real estate can be the ultimate solution for preserving an artist's work, this bonus just adds credence to the argument that artists from a very early point should seek long-term answers to their workspace, primarily by purchasing ample space for bargain prices.

Art Communities

MILL STORY

There are community arts-oriented buildings around the country-- take a search on Google. These are loft buildings that aim for people in the arts, by providing in addition to residential space, workspace, group exhibition space, and so forth.

When I did my "Donald Trump" project here in North Adams a decade ago by converting a 130,000 square foot mill building into 40 large (2,000 to 2,400 square foot average) live-work lofts, 60 artists (singles and couples) from around the country stampeded to buy into the project at bargain prices. That project has had a major impact upon the region and the artists have profited as the values of their lofts have almost double from the original purchase prices.

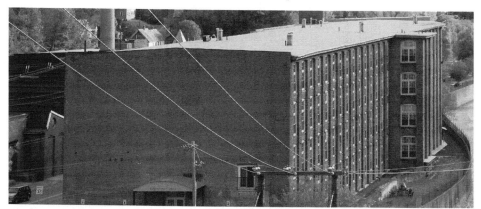

The Eclipse Mill Artist Lofts in North Adams, MA; 130,000 square foot divided into 40 large live/work lofts for artists. (photo by Kelly Lee)

One major requirement was that you had to be an artist to buy in. That, itself, made the building attractive for artists. The draw was more than just about space-- it was knowing that the building would consist of a creative community. I'm pretty sure, however, I would not have sold out so quickly nor would the loft project have been so attractive to artists had there been a minimum age requirement of 50 (for example), as many senior citizen communities have across the country.

In the Eclipse Mill, the initial buyers were artists from their late 20s into their mid 60s. However, there has been a turnover with an older age group of artists replacing those who have sold, mostly because the lofts are now more expensive and younger artists do not have the financial wealth to buy them. In addition, some of the middle-aged artists who were original buyers are now a decade older. This has shifted the average age to an "over 50 group." We joke that it is not a far-fetched thought that at some point, a meals-on-wheels wagon or a book-cart might get rolled down the hallways servicing the artists.

In many ways, the Eclipse Mill, by accident or by definition of a community loft building, is an ideal environment for the older artist, and although it has many limitations, it might be a very satisfying middle road for many artists to take. Their condo fees pay for all of the building's maintenance, including snow plowing the parking lot and keeping the exterior fit. There is an in-house gallery that is staffed, and other gallery spaces are available throughout the mill. The artists participate in many programs, including annual open-studios. So for an older artist, where a 2,400 square foot loft is ample space to live and work, and who wants limited chores of ownership, a condominium artist's loft is a viable option. (I mention this although I also have to warn you that condominiums and community living in general comes with many negatives. That is a personal decision.)

Although a condominium live/work loft might help through the older years, it does not address what happens upon death. However, just as I designed features to make the Eclipse Mill more attractive for artists - like galleries on each floor and extra wide halls so art can be displayed, a large first floor gallery geared for public exhibitions and large storage bins in the basement, as well as open loft space with double wide entrance doors, work sinks for messy cleanup, and proper lighting within the lofts - if I were to do the same project again but aimed at an older clientele, I might expand the development to include additional features.

For example, pretend I am developing the Eclipse Mill all over again and I want to attract senior artists. I could divide up the building differently, or take annex space in an adjacent building, to include an option for storage areas to be much larger, so that the artists could purchase storage rooms perhaps 10 x 10, 10 x 20 or 10 x 30 feet in size.

For a price that would include purchase of the second space, a one-time fee for recording each work that would go into the storage room (this would mean a digital photograph and description), and using part of the funds to set up an endowment that would pay for an exhibition every year in the main gallery comprised of works from these storage rooms, with the promise that each artist would have at least two works (or based on a specific square footage of floor or wall gallery space) exhibited no less than every two years, this development might not only allow artists to continue to work in their later years, but upon death, the artist would be assured that his or her work would continue to be stored and exhibited many years into the future. How much would that cost? It could be part of the sales price of the loft. Even if it added $50,000 or more, it would be a reasonable investment and alternative option for the artist.

Even more ambitious would be to expand this idea as a full-fledge museum space. For example, across the street from the Eclipse Mill is another mill, only two stories with very high ceilings, that has 200,000 square feet. It's enormous. I had the idea that a rich collector could renovate the mill and create a sensational museum for just a few million dollars. This amount sounds like a lot, but it's only a fraction of what it would cost to do such a museum in a major city. Since it is a half-mile from MASS MoCA and five miles from the Clark Art and Williams College Museum of Art, a proper collection could draw more than 50,000 visitors a year. That is almost a given, because MASS MoCA draws more than 100,000 visitors annually.

Obviously, the same museum with a less fancy renovation, and with unknown names might not draw even 10% of the visitation, but perhaps if it were also combined with other features, such as a café and a retail store, visitation would increase. Again, if 30 artists were curated into this museum space, and each paid a $50,000 purchase price for their storage space and exhibition services, that $1.5 million might make something like that happen.

The worry, and initial resistance that someone would have (and this thought would be the first thing that would enter my head) is that a developer would be doing this as a scam solely for profit and it would have no artistic value. However, if such a development had the sanction and participation of a major museum or major gallery/museum director, then all of a sudden artists would view the offering differently. If a major "name" artist participated, I would bet that many artists would be kicking down the door to participate.

It's often a matter of establishing the first one, and setting an example. To my knowledge, no one has done this type of ambitious project. However, keep in mind that what I'm talking about is way beyond a cooperative gallery. It is a joint venture but one that has to be curated to achieve the reputation that would be necessary, rather than have entry only by payment. Perhaps down the road, once several of these were started, variations would allow any artist to buy in.

So this picture of a large live/work condominium loft might fit many artists who can organize and compartmentalize their work into a suitable live/work space where the structure might be cared for by a monthly condo fee. And if the developer was creative and innovative, then these extra services could be offered with a (suggested) 50-year additional operation.

If this type space could then be financed and partnered in such a way that future maintenance and curatorial work would be supplied by a steady entity (a college, for example), then the artist's work could be preserved and exhibited into the future.

I'm just speculating, but based on my experience with developing the Eclipse Mill, I think something very close to this might work. The problem is, I'm out of the loft development business so we'll need to find an entrepreneur who has this type of imagination.

SNOWBIRDS

Artists move about, but not easily. It is not easy to pack up studio and work and set up in a new place. The older one is, the more 'stuff' there is to move. It's difficult enough to move across town, let alone move across the country.

But many seniors do downsize and move. The typical scene is to sell the house in the north and buy a condo in the south. Florida is the east coast retirement destination for many.

This discussion might all seem too obvious. We all have thought about where we'd like to live if we could choose any location, either has a permanent home or as a second home. Most people would choose a warmer climate with access to whatever pleases us-- beach, golf, mountains, or culture. Some will choose rural or resort; others will want to be in the heart of city life. But few artists should seek a change of location without considering how their art will fare, and how it might be preserved forever.

For artists, it's more than just having comfort and downsizing. Many artists need to upsize, if anything, for they can't give their art to Goodwill in order to downsize to a condo. And there are business considerations-- galleries or cultural stimulation and connections, and the ability to make and sell work. Artists do not retire the way most people do; they keep on working.

As we mature, our knowledge about how to get our work fabricated evolves. Artists will know the best place to get lumber, or to get someone to help make the stretchers, or weld some metal, and so forth. In the same light, artists might have a space that, over the years, has been designed and built around specific processes. This might mean special electrical hookups for equipment, customized exhaust systems, storage bins built for specific work and materials, and so forth. Take into consideration all of these elements, and it might take your breath away to think about moving and starting from scratch in a bare room.

Often, a solution might be in dividing up the year between two places. My wife and I now winter in Mexico. I haven't figured it out exactly because there are many variables, but I actually believe that we save money by going there. Before heading to warm weather, I shut down the heat where there's no water, and I turn down the thermostat in the other areas to 40 degrees. The heat savings alone, especially since we have such a large studio and loft, saves me a tremendous amount of money. In Mexico, we use no heat and no air conditioning - the weather is nearly perfect for the winter months. Mexico provides a stimulating environment because we are in a small beach town with a very liberal foreign community combined with the local population, but there are few cultural attractions like museums and theaters within reasonable driving distance. But that's not why we are there-- we go to enough exhibitions and performances during any given year, but fewer during our time in Mexico.

By residing in a second place, I'm faced with altering my work routine. For decades, I've worked pretty much the entire calendar year, except for travel time. For those winter months we now spend in Mexico, I can't create art in my gigantic studio, using all my materials. Instead, I have a small studio to do small work-- on paper mostly. But getting distance from my studio also has its advantages - I can get perspective on what I'm doing, I can catch my breath so I don't get burned out, I can plan large projects and have time for those odd-ball projects that I always seem to squeeze in, including doing various writing projects.

I live in a place with decent Internet, and so with basic art materials on a small scale, and my computer with communication abilities, I can stay in touch of what's going on, including operating my buildings in North Adams, while I do my art and writing-- all the while donning a T-shirt. So far, it's working out fine.

Perhaps this is a defensive mode; if I were rich and famous, the demand for my work might stimulate me to have assistants working full time. But since I'm a step or two below that level, I can leave for the winter and no assistant will suffer the loss of a job. Of course, wintering away is a 'work in progress,' and we'll see if I feel the need to do something different. Obviously, I have the option to return to my main studio earlier and do work, so I have not permanently burned my bridges. But for those artists who choose to follow a path towards the south on a permanent basis, or even to move to another region for personal, family, economic or cultural reasons, the move must be well thought out, because it is often impossible to return.

Sometimes wishes are just not practical. I had a few shows in California many years ago, and I was drawn to that culture, as I was tiring of the political nature of Washington D.C.   Wetting my appetite, curators in California seemed to accept my style of work much more readily than eastern curators. The technologies that I was working with fitted right in with the Hollywood/LA mentality. Plus, a side incentive was to take advantage of the (then) great public university system for our kids. But to secure 10,000 to 20,000 square feet of studio space on the West Coast would have required me to be a multi-millionaire. We looked, but I just couldn't find any affordable combination. Huge industrial space on the East Coast was practically free by comparison.

When we moved from Washington D.C. to North Adams in the Berkshires, I went from big city to small town. Two decades later, I can tell you one thing-- it would be difficult to try to return to Washington, not just because the art movement has moved on and my connections and friends have died, retired, or moved on themselves, but because a decent but modest house in the District will cost $1 million. That's at least five times the cost of an equivalent house in North Adams! Basically, wherever I went during my most recent visit to Washington, I had sticker shock. It was difficult to think that I once had a townhouse and huge studio there. If I had stayed, however, they would be worth a lot but I'd be paying more in taxes, more in transportation, more in most anything we'd do, and my wife and I would be working harder to maintain the income to keep up.

I also wrote a decade ago about how much easier it is to live in a small town compared to a large city. When I used to need my equipment repaired, it would be a trek in traffic across the city that would easily eat up a half day. Here, in North Adams, help is no more than five minutes away and there is never a line. I felt this advantage upon moving here as a bonus, but as I have aged, I now feel this convenience as a necessity. I have less patience in dealing with the strain of city living, and I find I have more time to do what I choose to do, including studio work. Again, there are many sides to this; some artists can't live away from the big city, and others tolerate big cities in short visits - while others want both, and divide their time between two places.

So there are tradeoffs.   Artists, like almost anyone considering retirement, might look to more attractive places to live. Many web sites offer "the best small towns" or "the best small cities" to live, and many have cultural features that might attract artists. But the considerations are immense, and much more complicated for the artist over the average retiree, because the artist is moving not only family but 'the business.'

For our Mexico choice, I made a list and it provided check marks on most of my needs. There were cheaper places to go, like a number of countries in Asia (where fabrication labor was attractive for some of my projects), but the distance and even difficulty in shipping back artwork, ruled out those possibilities.

Like any "retiree" considering a second home and not just thinking about art, I wanted a place near a major airport to make getting back and forth as easy as possible. We wanted medical care with doctors and hospitals; we wanted Internet service; we wanted someplace safe (and yes, Mexico is safe - we are in a small town near a major resort city, but a thousand miles away from the border cities where most of the problems occur; Mexico is generally safer than the U.S.); we wanted a place where we could buy enough space for family and friends and a small studio; we wanted a place that had character and was interesting, we wanted someplace warm (I might have chosen other places, perhaps in Italy, but we needed a place that was warm for the specific time we wanted to be away- which meant the five winter months). Upon our first visit to the town, we couldn't find an affordable house and we were about to leave, thinking it wasn't "meant to be." But at the last moment, we found a hillside lot and an architect/builder finishing a house next door, and it just sort of fell into place. That's the way it is sometimes- but you have to be ready to jump at the opportunity. We did all that in a week's visit and didn't come back until the house was half built. A bit chancy but it turned out fine. We chose Mexico as an escape destination, as a second-home/studio and not as a place to live year-round. My reasoning was simple: if it didn't work out, we could sell and think about a different location; our home base was intact.

For other artists, two places might work as much as staying, or as much as moving lock stock and barrel to another part of the country. All solutions can be good, if the particular specifics support your goals.

At one point, I almost moved family into my studio, eliminating the need for a separate house altogether. The income freed up by this condensing could have been applied for another space somewhere else. Certainly, my heat savings is common to anyone who goes south for the winter.

The south is not free. For example, space in southern humid areas would have to be air conditioned unless you want your art to disintegrate in just a few years from the humidity, so that is a major expense and worry.   In the north, I found cheap industrial buildings for bargain prices, and cold does not damage art in most cases, just moisture. So if you keep things dry, you should be fine. I have 50,000 square feet full of art that is mostly in cold space during winter months, and I've been fine for more than 22 years so far. So those assets far outweighed the negatives, and our solution was to be based in the north and escape to a warmer destination during the five expensive winter months, rather than to move permanently to the south.

MORE ABOUT AN ARTIST COMMUNITY

Artist communities can have a major impact on the nation's art scene. All over, there are real estate wastelands as major chain stores, motels, movie theaters and retail businesses have exited the downtowns of towns and cities across the country in favor of malls and commercial strips in the outskirts, where the land is cheaper and more abundant for their gigantic complexes.   Americans almost live in their cars, and parking has become the key ingredient in all large retail businesses.

So we have ample available spaces that have been deserted or underutilized. We have towns desperate for occupants and activity. And we have a burgeoning art community.   What's missing is a governmental program that tries to give the initial funding to bring these components together and to make things happen. This is a major failure of the National Endowment for the Arts, as well as many state arts councils.

Nevertheless, if more examples could be attempted, the successful pilot programs would prove their worth and become models for the rest of the country and perhaps, a movement could then take off.

The idea is that artists (visual and performing) want a place to live and a place to work that is stimulating. They need an audience. Historically, once an area achieves critical mass, it becomes a lively arts district and all kinds of restaurants and boutiques and tourists soon follow. This is basic urban planning with a proven track record. Now it's time to apply these principles to underused areas of our country, where "deferred maintenance" is the most polite way to talk about the condition of the properties.

The Eclipse Mill building is one of the more successful buildings for artists in the nation. It had a cultural magnet (MASS MoCA and other museums in the Berkshires) but North Adams was an untested town for loft development. It was dicey also because many other loft buildings were not as successful as their PR brochures would imply.

Generally, the track records of other artist buildings are mixed. Many were done with the best of intentions, but when the numbers didn't quite work out, compromises were accepted. For example, many lofts were sold to the lawyer-types who simply wanted to live in an arty environment. Lofts then became so fashionable that regular apartments are now advertised as lofts just to help sell them. The artists took a back seat because their subsidized rents or prices couldn't justify the costs.

Other buildings were more restrictive in accepting tenants, but many of these are rental buildings. Most of the federal and state tax laws favor developers doing low-income rental buildings. Artists generally fit within the income requirements of low-income. Even though condominium ownership attracts a better community of folks because they have 'invested' into the community and have incentives to get involved with making the region better, due to tax credits and tax incentives for low-income rental housing as well as increased taxes on short term capital gains, the developer is essentially penalized for selling the loft units as condominiums, rather than renting. That is why there are few condominium loft buildings adhering to strict art standards.

Ownership is better for the artist, because appreciation and paying off the mortgage gives that person options for the future. A rental traps that person. In twenty years, if the artist wants to move, he or she has to start all over but most likely at much higher costs for ownership or renting another loft. Renting in the long run is a fool's game, even if the rents are subsidized and given to artists for under-market rates. Nevertheless, many buildings that are geared for artists will only allow rentals. In fairness, some buildings try very hard to keep the quality up of artist-tenants and also they try to keep the rents affordable, but I still don't think it's a recipe that will benefit artists in the long run.

The Eclipse Mill was sold at low, affordable prices. I developed a unique method of renovating the mill under what I called a "mean and lean" mentality. Since then, the artists who purchased the units have realized at least a $100,000 profit. The ones who sold have that money in their pocket to use for their new purchase. The ones who still own their units have that appreciation and can borrow against it in case of emergency. Meanwhile, the mill maintains a strict admission process. In order to move in (and this is true if a loft is rented out or sold), the tenant must show a professional bio and exhibition record in order to be accepted. To my knowledge, they try not to judge on whether they like the work or not, but only if the applicant has a track record of professional showing and working.

While one can be critical in various ways, so far it's working fairly well. One negative is that while valuations go up, so too go property taxes. And as values go up, the average age goes up-- that can be a negative or that fact can be purposely factored in. In any case, with older artists currently moving into the building, coupled with the number of artists who have been there from day one but are now ten years older, the general resident population is now "up there" in age.

Fifty is pretty young, and being 60 or so is not so old! It's not like the building is full of artists on their last legs! They are so active that they hold gallery exhibitions and open-studios in the building and are engaged in hundreds of other ways within the region. Since the artists are mature, they know what they want and they know how to go about getting things done. So while AARP would be pleased with the resident artists, it is certainly not a building for artists waiting to expire.

So in this light, I see many more such buildings being done, and with services aimed for older artists added on.

If you combine these ideas, it seems logical to me that a new model for the mature artist can be produced, and if governmental arts agencies can get behind this concept and spearhead it for distressed communities, this type of model program can become a national trend and have a tremendous impact on artists across the country.

First Step: Preservation

KEEPING YOUR ART SAFE (OR SAFER)

Another issue for senior artists to deal with, that should be dealt with sooner rather than later, is documentation of the work. This means digitizing all photos of the artwork, as well as having descriptions gathered in a sensible file that easily can be accessed by whoever is appointed.

These aspects affect all artists, and each artist's work will thrive or not after the artist's death, depending on related circumstances.

I'll bet that if you are over 50, you photographed your early work with film, and now you have hundreds of slides of your work. Well, have you digitized them? I've tried, but so far, I'm not the one to boast. I must have two or three thousand slides of my work. I'm still looking out for that person whom I can hire at $10 per hour to spend hundreds of hours putting slides onto a scanner and getting digitized images into a secure computer file system. That's a necessary task, but if I have the $1,000 to $5,000 to spend, I have many other priorities. The lazier I feel, the more that chore will be dumped upon someone at my death-- but that's not really fair. Thankfully, the equipment has improved and there are now companies to whom you can send boxes of your slides and who will digitize them for you for between 22 to 50 cents per slide.

Preservation efforts usually are included in 'what we'll do tomorrow but not today' list. I have thousands of works that I haven't looked at in decades. I don't have the time. I tell myself that I could spend all my working time just dealing with my art from the past -- repairing, preserving, re-wrapping, better storing, documenting, etc. I have come across plastic-wrapped paintings so old that the plastic is crumbling. It's not something I want to get into because I know if I start with a few, it will end up being a bottomless pit, and I don't want to go there. In addition, for those works that were already put away, I never wrote a real list and details about what I was putting away. I might have memory of them if I saw them today - at least I think so - but part of my purpose in going through my storage would be to just document what I have with a proper description so that anyone who goes through the storage will know what I have and when they were done and have titles, and so forth. This is just basic stuff that any museum would have, but few artists who operate alone have such a good record. If your work was selling in the six figures, then yes, the galleries would insist and you'd have it all done by studio office assistants. For the 99% of artists, however, this is a nightmare that has been "deferred."

So I avoid even thinking about these things most of the time. I'm sure I'm not alone. With limited resources, how much time and money and effort do I want to put into my past, rather than to realize future projects?

DOCUMENTATION AND FILM

I recently saw a couple of new documentary films about contemporary artists. In reality, it's quite a compliment for an artist when someone wants to do a film about you. But the reality is that the potential audience is small. It's not comparable to a popular movie or TV show where there are millions of viewers. If you are lucky, it might be seen in a few film festivals, by some art schools or art departments of colleges, perhaps shown before some art groups, and the biggie would be on PBS or other national cable shows.

The value of a properly done film, however, is priceless in the years to come, if you want the public to know about you, how you went about doing work, and so forth. Keep in mind, films have a shelf life and usually it's only beneficial the first year that it's released. Nevertheless, it's invaluable for long-term archival purposes. However, for it's use after you are dead, it will have limited value unless there is a plan for its use.

Someone did a film about me thirty-five years ago; it shows its age; and it's not digitized. Years ago, I did put effort into transferring it from film to VHS tape in order to make it available for an exhibition. But In all the years since DVDs been around, I've not spent the time to transfer it once again. I just can't spend my entire life to preserve or document or deal with all this-- I'm like all of you, I just want someone to do it all for me upon my death. It's not going to happen; I know that just as you know that no one is going to care about your stuff unless you do what I'm just beginning to do-- take the initiative. Make a plan and a "to do" list and work towards your goal each year.

For example, to my credit, I did write a summary of my art development. It numbered about 35 pages, as I went through, from memory, most of my art "periods." I explained why I got into whatever I did, what materials or processes I used, how it might have been shown, etc. I'm hoping that if a young curator ever wants to learn about my art, this summary will give him/her a good overview. It will put into context whatever work someone happens to come across. So where to keep even that? It's currently in my computer. Do I assume that someone will know to save my computer folders and find this particular file, if I should die tomorrow? Should I print out a copy and leave it somewhere that for sure won't be missed by my next of kin? Do I put this in a bank security box? Is this the most important thing to mark as "important, do not throw away?" -- or to mark "in event of death?" Or should it just be one of dozens of artifacts, including show announcements, catalogs that I'm in, correspondence, slides, videos, reviews in magazines and newspapers, etc. - all that should be put into a box and carefully stored with instructions?

Am I foolishly imagining that someone will have the wherewithal and incentive to go through all my papers and fish out the important papers to archive?

For about two years in the early 1970s, I constructed large wall reliefs consisting of large planks. The planks were composed on the wall, scattered and overlapped, and each wall grouping had to be installed with dowels into custom-made wall receivers. To position the receivers correctly, I had a full-scale drawing (like a blue print), so that would be taped to the wall, and then the positions marked. First the custom-made receiver blocks would be screwed to the wall at the marked spots; then dowels of various lengths had to be inserted and then into the planks, in a certain order and method. I remember I typed up instructions because I sold a few out of the area and the installer of the gallery or perhaps the purchaser needed to have that information in order to 'hang' the art.

All the planks, drawings, receivers, dowels, etc have all been put into boxes and in various places when I moved to my current studio. I haven't used them in almost three decades, and I haven't even seen them since moving here 22 years ago. They were marked, in some way, I remember. If I were to find and assemble them, I'm sure I could do it within a reasonable time period, because I'm familiar with them. After all, I made them. But who, in the future, will be able to figure out which plank goes to what piece and then find the matching blueprint, and then put it all together? If my name was "Picasso," I'm sure the museum conservation staff could assemble the proper intelligence team and make it happen-- but in a practical sense, do I expect the one person who might want to do something (if I'm lucky) will have the time and resources to preserve and resurrect my work? Will this be a directive from my widow? From my children? In reality, it's a very risky bet.

I warned you in advance that some solutions I know about not because I can offer you easy solutions, but because I can share with you, and therefore point out to you the problems we all have. I know the solutions; I just need to emphasize that they're not easy because this work is not going to happen automatically. If you do nothing, you'll be OK because you'll be dead; you won't know. But while you are alive, you should realize that your art has a much better chance of ending up in the dumpster unless you do something about it.

It's a shame that more efforts are not put into documenting an artist or other people in the arts while they are alive. Documentary films are really a treasure. So are books that reveal what can never be learned second-hand.

For example, I remember when my friend Walter Hopps passed away. He was one of the most brilliant museum directors in the contemporary art world. At his memorial in Houston, I mentioned that someone should organize a book about him, with essays being submitted from his friends, colleagues and artists whom he dealt with. Memories were fresh at the time; but imagine if that project had started a few years earlier when he was still alive. What a wonderful manuscript it could have been to have a few pages written by Rauschenberg or Keinholtz, as examples. I would have written a wonderful story about him, as would scores of other artists whom I know. Walter was the most unique curator and museum director ever, combining genius with an obsession to keeping up with every detail of the artists he respected and befriended. Those artists and art professionals could have described his working approaches in ways that no scholar will ever discover decades from now.

Perhaps too many books about too many artists will overload the system. Just contemplating all the books that have been written by people about their lives must be daunting. Of course, 99.9% are not going to have historical value beyond the writer's family, but in the case of someone who worked with famous artists and renowned museums, I can imagine a book being devoured by every ambitious art history student who wants to curate shows. But it's been quite a few years, and some of the people who could have written about Walter are gone themselves, and others are not capable of writing their essays as they might have been several years ago. Memories fade, and what we learn in history textbooks that will be written someday will mostly be dry information found by written research—not the juicy stuff that brings it all alive.

I think about these things, as I observe many interesting occurrences that in retrospect have historical interest. Yet no one is properly documenting this stuff.

So it goes with most artists. Artists who don't write or aren't savvy about making videos will miss an opportunity to translate their art processes and careers into other media. If the artists can't do it for themselves, then it's great if someone takes an interest in doing it, but that's rare. Perhaps the art can speak for itself, but usually art will be better appreciated, by a larger audience, if there are supporting materials that explain what really went on.

As artists get older, they understand more fully their involvement during a whole era of art history. A half-century or more of working covers quite a spread of what has happened in art over the centuries. More specifically, an artist's career certainly covers in detail a regional development—whether it's the association with a city or state or an artistic style. Putting the artist's art in historical context was always important to Walter Hopps, and I am trying to stimulate other artists to think about their work through the same lens that he would have used. Think of your art as historically important; then determine how that should be documented.

PRESERVING WORK

Preservation is thankless work. It's not exciting and it's not about creating something new. It's more about wrapping and storing and repairing. I'm not the best role model and I'm not the goody-good person who practices what I preach. However, it's terrible when I discover that my art has been damaged because I was too lazy to spend five minutes to wrap something up with plastic. And after storing works for two or more decades, where some of my wrapping materials have begun to crumble upon being touched, I could spend a full month with a team of three assistants going through my work - cleaning, wrapping and recording what I have. I'm like all of you in thinking that if I just 'kick the can' a bit and put off until tomorrow, someone else will manage that boring task.

It's not right and at some point soon, I'll have to compartmentalize the work, buckle down for a few days and try to make a dent. It's like most boring tasks - once you get through some of the tasks and set up a system, the next time becomes easier. But if you don't start soon, the work will not get easier when you are much older.

All works should be wrapped in plastic, shielded from light and dust and water, and stored carefully. Drawings should be in flat drawers that are also dust-free. Three-dimensional works also need to be covered or wrapped, and stored.

All works should be properly marked with date, title, material and size, and this should be stored in a computer file system, preferably with a photo.

The task of preservation involves pretty basic stuff but more geared for the professional office person rather than for the 'crazy artist.' However, as I've pointed out, a serious artist needs to have two attitudes. One characteristic can be as wild as the artist wants in creating art, but when it comes to cutting wood on a power saw, that same artist needs a completely different mental state unless the artist wants to join the many who have fewer than ten fingers. Preservation needs that same rationale - calm attitude coupled with discipline to get the chore done.

In almost every estate that I've known about or read about, the first task by the executor, often the spouse or children, has been to do an inventory of all the art. No one can deal with the art unless they know what is involved. This has been done for estates that have value and interest. Unfortunately, the dumpster and basement have taken care of the majority of art estates.

The Artist's Estate: Options

CREATE YOUR OWN STORAGE AND EXHIBIT SPACE - SMALL MODEL

During the artist's lifetime, storage demands will increase. Hopefully, this space is purchased and over a few decades, it might be completely paid for. Then the question is, what are future maintenance, tax and utility expenses?

In my examples, I propose to you that you set up a non-profit foundation-corporation that would enable you to apply for 501c3 status. This would mean that friends and supporters could donate to your foundation and have it be tax deductible. It would also mean that you could avoid paying real estate taxes on the space that's used for foundation purposes. However, there are set-up fees and annual filing fees that have to be paid. But let's say that you did this and let's apply this structure to a few types of possibilities.

If you like the idea that your art will survive in a special place after you die, then the most logical concept is that your studio could be turned into permanent storage and exhibition space. As part of the exhibition, educational elements could show how you worked and put your art into historical context. However, not all studios can be turned into public spaces, due to zoning or practical aspects, such as access and costs.

There are areas where houses have been built for personal art collections, which turn into public museums after the owners passed on. In some cases, like the Clark Art Institute in Williamstown, MA or the Kreeger Museum in Washington D.C., the residences were built with a museum in mind. Other homes of famous artists are now museums, but these are usually reserved for those superstars who are considered national treasures.

Nevertheless, as artists move to new studios, this concept can be kept in mind. A space or building or studio in a commercially zoned area, directly on commercial streets with handicapped access - versus in a back alley or a second or third floor walkup above a store - would better serve as a place that could be turned from studio to mini-museum.

While a space exclusively for exhibition purposes could be considered, the idea that the artist can make use of the space during his or her lifetime, encourages that space to be a studio first, and then turned into exhibition space after the artist's death. Not all commercial spaces, however, that would be good for public display space, will be adequate for a studio-- it depends on what your town's zoning says about manufacturing. A retail jeweler usually will have a repair shop in the back, where the owner can also make original pieces, and no zoning officer would probably care. But an artist creating large-scale work, perhaps using sprays and woodworking equipment, might need to be in an area zoned for light industrial. On the other hand, many residential areas are fine for an artist's studio because the artist is usually not doing the quantity of work that would bother neighbors. In addition, most cities have zoning that allows for home businesses. All I can tell you is that being an artist usually puts you in a grey area between these designations, and before you make permanent plans and investment, it's best to carefully check it out and get permits or permission in writing.

Still, the studio is a natural place to combine your current needs as well as have it continue to support your art after you are gone. So when selecting your next studio, especially if you are in your later years, you might want to give careful thought to how you will protect your work after you are gone.

WHAT DO YOU NEED TO RUN A MINIATURE ART MUSEUM OF YOUR WORK?

Lets quickly examine the basic ingredients necessary for creating a public display space, conservation lab and storage facility for the purpose of preserving the art after the artist has died.

Space: Space is at the heart of any plan. A fifty-year lease can possibly work, but space that is owned free and clear is the best. You can create a public exhibition facility in a very modest space-- a couple of hundred square feet for storage and a few hundred square feet for exhibition (a bathroom or access to a bathroom helps) - really not much different in size or scope than any number of private art galleries throughout the United States. The difference? You aren't necessarily trying to sell, although a permanent show room of art that is for sale could be an alternative option. The big factor is that all galleries are staffed. The gallery's goal is to attract visitors and then to close on sales-- that takes a personal touch in most cases, although online sales are affecting galleries in the same way as they are affecting other retail stores. In this case, it is to preserve and display the art of an artist, not necessarily to sell it.

I stress that space is at the heart of carrying out your plans. Having it be affordable, be accessible, and be manageable should be at the forefront of your search.

Staff: Are there ways to have a gallery open with no staff? Who is going to open and shut the front door? Can the art be seen properly from a stationary point, perhaps through a protective glass barrier, without entering? And if operating the art space depends on staffing, how can one ensure that you will always have someone without having an administrative structure in place to arrange, pay and deal with employee issues?

A partnership with an organization that might staff an adjoining space might be of use; but there's little assurance that the alliance will last more than a year or two, based on traditional business records. Partnering with a school or small museum would be a much better bet.

As a last resort, your foundation will have to hire someone, and then you'll need a manager to oversee that, because few staff people will last more than a year or two.

A manager: There are agencies, but again, if you are not around and the agency with which you have made arrangements goes out of business, you'll still need a legal structure with money behind it that will have the authority and ability to replace whatever system for staffing you put into place.

In my case, I've begun having discussions with the nearby college where an arts management program could supply an ample number of students. But they will not be that interested in your venture unless the quality of the art and the financial rewards are enticing. Most colleges are looking for intern opportunities for their students, and paid internships are valuable. If you offer enough, I'm sure you can make a deal.

So caring for a museum's operation falls upon the foundation's board, and then the appointed managers; some will work for free if there's a personal desire; most will work by the billable hour. It's beneficial, of course, if the artist makes these arrangements while alive.

Curatorial expertise: This kind of expertise is not easy to find, and not easy to keep. Again, few will have the luxury or desire to work for free. However, unless your instructions are ironclad (and few are), someone who has artistic judgment will have to tinker with how your art is presented to the public.

Utilities: This just concerns routine stuff, but someone has to pay the bills, be there to maintain heating and electrical systems, and even change the light bulbs. Again, service contracts are great, as long as the contractor stays in business. When something has to change, it will fall upon the manager and/or the trustee to make it happen. The real issue is, who will be there to notice and to then call the plumber when the ceiling is dripping with water?

Preservation and maintenance details: I'm assuming that not all your art can be exhibited at one time. Therefore, the rest of the art has to be wrapped, stored, cared for, and then unwrapped and exhibited, while other pieces go back into storage. This is not a task that can be contracted out to an outfit in the telephone book; it needs some careful handling; in other words, it needs someone who is used to handling art.

Financial and legal oversight: Unfortunately, lawyers and accountants are expensive and they bill by the hour. There are ways for the artist to get knowledgeable about how to form a foundation/structure before having to hire the staff, and there are ways to make sure those expenses are capped on an annual basis. However, since you, the artist, won't be around for when all this is going on, it's tough to avoid these expenses at some point.

Organizational structure to allow all of the above: An organization has to be formed to be the legal entity to carry out your wishes. The most probable (but there are alternatives) organization is an educational foundation that you should have formed prior to your death in order to receive, preserve and exhibit your art and generally to make it available to the public.

Whoever is doing the legal and financial work, is the logical person or firm to continue, except for one thing-- you are making plans for an operation that will take many years to implement and will continue (hopefully) for many years thereafter. Those folks won't be around someday, as you won't be around. You can try to make arrangements with a young firm/lawyer/accountant, but there are no guarantees in life.

The idea of having a foundation as the entity that will oversee the museum operation is fine, as long as you have enough money in the bank for it to be self-sufficient - so that board members can be replaced as necessary and proper oversight can be hired. This is not something that can be done on the cheap-- legal and financial folks cost an arm and a leg.

General: Goals, oversight of operation: What happens if no one comes? When should the towel be thrown in? Who is going to oversee the overall operation, and determine whether your plans are working? What happens if no one comes, if it's just too expensive to operate, if there are unforeseen expenses? Someone has to be able to alter plans and even to end them.

Alternative distribution and exhibition plans: A reasonable approach, unless you have millions in assets (liquid and art) is to draw up plans but have various levels-- or plans A, B, C and so forth. If all goes well, instigate one type of operation; if income is less and expenses are greater, stipulate the use of a scaled back operation. And you can even have a backup to a backup plan, with a minimum operation should your initial systems fail.

It's possible to take your plans and stretch them over a longer time-line. After all, you'll be dead and so you'll have more patience than when you were alive. For my personal plans, I am prepared to initiate a fairly affordable operation with minimum activities. During a period of minimum operation, reserves can be built up, unused space can be rented out, and expenses minimized in order to stay in business. At some point, when interest and assets build up, the operation can be expanded.

NEGATIVES DO NOT OVERWEIGH THE POSITIVE

I'm trying to put the reality in front of you, mostly in the form of the finances such an undertaking will demand and the public interest it might not receive even if you go to the trouble and expense of forming such a foundation. There's no reason to have unrealistic expectations about the undertaking. In my judgment, however, these negatives do not overweigh the positive.

If you have ten years to prepare and only a few thousand dollars in cash assets, somewhere in the United States and probably not more than two hours away from where you currently live, you can secure space and a program that would carry out your wishes to preserve your work and make it available for many years into the future. It might be a very modest operation, and a cultural venue might seem out of character where you locate, but the point is that even if you do it on a very modest scale, it will have meaning and longevity. The more artists who join this movement, the more interesting it will become.

However, if you overreach, you can stretch your financial abilities too far until your project collapses. That's a real danger. Only by taking careful precautionary measures can you prevent this from happening.

MAKE IT DIFFERENT; MAKE IT EDUCATIONAL

Not only should your art be good enough to be preserved and exhibited for future generations, but how that is done will be equally important. I've curated many shows during my career, including the ten years I was founder-director of the Contemporary Artists Center. I was taught by the best, including the late museum director Walter Hopps, who was considered by many as one of the top ten curators in the world. I know that when you consider exhibiting your work, especially for a permanent exhibition, it has to be done "right." A good installation can make art look like a million dollars; a bad installation can make art look worse than a student art show.

It should also hold up in other ways. You are not only addressing the current audience, but the idea is to address a future audience - one that will have new design experiences. Doing it differently, almost like it's own art installation, might give the display the zing it needs.

If your art is on display, then the opportunity exists to put forth some educational aspects. It's important that viewers understand the 'what' and the 'why.' Lay audiences often think of contemporary art as one big joke being played on them. That's an easy fix. Explanations need not be boring text pasted on the gallery wall. With iPads and computers, there are many easy interactive ways to explain what the art is about. This also becomes the time you can put it all in historical context. Perhaps you want to also reveal your other work by reference, your processes, your struggles, your uniqueness-- all this can be done through video, audio and power point-like label displays.

Your explanations can be geared for all levels- and each audience can choose which to access. There can be something for children, for the "non-art" person, as well as for the person who is well versed in art. You can also address viewers with different abilities by adjusting the manner in which you display the art and information, and you can have it all translated for the hearing impaired as well as translated into different languages. Again, all this is easy enough once you have defined your project.

Artists dream of having a curator who has genuine interest in their art, takes all of the above into consideration and puts forth all the resources that a major museum might have. But this is just a dream. However, when artists assume the role of curator, all these components and all this work still needs to be applied. Not all artists make good curators; if they don't have this skill, then they need to seek out young curators with incentives. Staging an exhibition is a partnership between good art and good curatorial knowledge.

Museum art exhibitions at mid-century looked quite different than if the same art were exhibited today. Curators today have new approaches to presenting the same material. At the same time, some contemporary art that might have been revered when first exhibited has not held up, while other works that are recognized today were less recognized in its day.

When you plan your museum space, first try to be very objective about your art. Is it as good as anything being done today? Will experts agree? Will it hold up in a decade, and even in a century?

Then treat your art as if you were the curator in the Museum of Modern Art. Present it professionally.

ONCE A COMMERCIAL STORE, NOW A MUSEUM

For sale, cheap - a small commercial store. Buy it? In my town, just a block or two away from MASS MoCA but in the midst of the downtown, you can purchase 1,000 square feet of commercial space for as little as $50,000. Using it and then paying off the mortgage, you'd still have some continued expenses. Either you'd pay some upkeep or you'd have to pay a condo fee if it were part of a larger commercial complex. In either case, let's say that basic fees with utilities cost you $200 a month. For $2,400 a year, you could operate an exhibition space of sorts, perhaps with 2/3 being for exhibition and 1/3 being for storage, bathroom, office. But who is going to run it?

Now we have to use our imaginations.

A store-turned-art-gallery in North Adams, MA. This one is for sale for $50,000.

Pretend that it is easy to see a large work through a retail window. You could craft a curtain and as they used to do in the old days when a giant masterpiece of Niagara Falls, for example, would go on national tour and visitors would pay ten cents and be admitted behind the red velvet curtain where the masterpiece would be on display, you could charge admission. Why not do the same? Create a coin box so when two quarters are inserted, the curtain would part and the viewer would have 5 minutes to view your installation. That would allow your space to be operated without a staff. Then you would only need to hire someone to make sure all is in working order, to empty the coin box, and to change the installation annually, dust, change light bulbs, etc. Remember, this is an amusing example, but one where aspects, perhaps, can be applied to a serious undertaking.

Alternatively, perhaps the space is only to be viewed from outside the picture window.   Maybe you want it seen for free, but with limited access; certainly at night, all lit up, it will have a great effect. Many years ago, a sculptor rented a tiny space with a very large retail window; he put two of his sculptures on a rotating base, and displayed his work. He had a web address in case anyone was interested in contacting him. A rotating platform or wall could be a way to show additional work when the viewer is in a stationary position.

Let's continue to explore the options with my commercial-store-turned-mini-art-museum.

Pretend that you endow the local college to run your exhibition space for the summer months. This could be an endowment that would be slowly used up, or an endowment where the interest earnings would pay for interns and modest supervision for the next fifty years. Then someone could follow your instructions and change the exhibition annually (assuming that change invites repeat visitors) and staff it with an actual person. If the space were open to the public for 30 hours per week, at $10 (rounded off), that's $300 times the number of weeks-- so if for a 12-week season, that's $4,600 a year needed to keep your mini-museum space open.

Now it doesn't take a rocket scientist to see that if two, three, or more artists combined their efforts, one staff person could cover a number of different spaces if they were all in the same complex with common entrance.

That's why I've been proposing to artists that they think collectively about these possibilities. What's wrong with having alternatives to large museums? Certainly, as downtowns have emptied out with chain stores and businesses moving to the outskirts, space for cultural projects has become more affordable.

FOR COLLECTORS; HAVING YOUR ART SEEN AND PROMOTED AFTER YOU'RE GONE

In most ways, there's not a lot of difference between an artist who has retained 200 works of art and a collector who has purchased 200 works of art. Both have to be stored and the question remains, what will happen upon later years and after the collector's and artist's death?

At what point does the collector deal with how the works get distributed? Will family members take over the assets? Will the art go to various museums? Will they simply get split up and sold the best way a dealer, estate attorney or family member can handle it?

And my question is-- should the collection be split up? If not, then are there museums that will take the collection as a donation, agree not to split it up or sell off valuable ones? Would the museum then agree to exhibit the collection either permanently or often enough to make the gift worthwhile.

And for those collections that have some regional interest but not enough to entice a museum, what happens?

As I will describe throughout the book, opting to keep the collection intact, and creating a home for the collection as a private museum, would be my recommendation.

First of all, I like oddball museum collections. I think a collection can have more character compared to homogenized museums that have a sampling of the same artists as most other museums have.

Second, there really is less of a reason to sell off the collection . With alternative and imaginative strategies, having a billion dollars is not necessary. One can create a museum and keep it running on a reasonable amount of money. So why not do it?

If the collector has the wherewithal to build up a substantial collection, that same bullish attitude is perfect when making a stand for the collection. It is not for the timid, but I've met no real collector who was timid. Scouting, making decisions, making deals with galleries, getting to know the artists, and knowing the business of money and art well enough to make decisions about purchasing - all this requires a certain street-sense. This experience is perfect for taking the next step.

WHO DECIDES?

Who chooses art from older artists for museums? We all know the incongruities of the art world. Many very good artists don't achieve fame, and some sneak in perhaps undeserving. I have made the case, however, that most artworks in the major museums are very good--- they deserve to be there. But we all know of artists who should also be in the collection and shown, but are left out. There are actually quite a few artists in the collections of museums, but most are not on view; most likely their work is in the basement storage. Nevertheless, the total number of artists represented in museums is a tiny fraction of the total number of respectable artists working today. Many more deserve to be included. Why some artists get the limelight and others don't has a lot more to do with curators, luck, connections, timing, money - and not just with the actual quality of the art.

Even with museums all over the country, the number of artists who produce competent art far outnumber the capacity of museums to include more than a tiny fraction of the work produced. What qualifies one artist's work over another? (Photo: Lincoln Gallery; Smithsonian American Art Museum.)

Getting recognized and getting your art into important collections is an ongoing aim for all artists, no matter the age. However, as we get older, we realize that our future time is shrinking and our connections might even be getting weaker, not stronger.

Older artists do not get "called" often; we are more a part of the woodwork than we once were-- gallery dealers and museum curators are looking for new talent and the 'new look.' If you are not a "name" already, the chance of being discovered late in life is next to nil. And even if you established a good reputation, the requests to exhibit your art will steadily decrease.

I mention all this in both my books but in the decade since I wrote those words, I have felt this even more. Once in a while a perk or some recognition appears. For example, a sculptor who was given a chance to curate a show for the San Francisco Museum of Modern Art, explored the museum's entire database of 7,000 paintings and sculptures, and he chose 25 works by 22 artists from the collection. I almost didn't spot my name on the exhibition announcement that arrived in the mail, but when I did, I was extra pleased to see that "Eric Rudd" was alphabetically sandwiched between Diego Rivera and George Segal. My wife and I flew out for the opening and after-party; it was bittersweet as several artists came up to me and admired my large work-- as if I had just created it in my studio. I held back from mentioning that the work was made 35 years earlier, probably before they were born! Keep in mind, it's gratifying to have my work in such an important museum collection, but it has been in their storage facility; the work did not see the light of day (or of an exhibition flood light) for more than three decades after the museum received the work. It might not see light again in my lifetime.

This work is in the collection of the San Francisco Museum of Modern Art, and was shown in an exhibition called "Not New Work" curated by sculptor Vincent Fecteau. The work was made in 1974, and had been in the collection for 30 years before it was chosen for this show.

As such opportunities come less frequently now, I therefore put more effort into making my own destiny - as you will read! I think there are many opportunities for older artists, but the earlier one starts, the easier!

Too bad they don't mention these things in art school!

ARE YOU GOOD ENOUGH FOR ANYONE TO CARE?

This is an important question, but very difficult for you or anyone to honestly and objectively answer. Let me try to draw an obvious difference. For example, if you are a hobbyist, and you normally show in craft fairs and shopping mall community exhibitions-- perhaps you'll admit to yourself that your work does not belong - now or even someday - in the collection of the Museum of Modern Art in New York. Now at some point, you might simply draw a list of friends that you could bequeath works to, and perhaps figure out how you'll distribute or dispose of your works upon your death. As a hobbyist, I doubt that your works number in the hundreds, and certainly not thousands. (Although there are "hobbyists" and then there are "dedicated hobbyists," so one never knows.)

If you are pretty famous already, and enough of your work has been distributed to museums and collections, perhaps you have less reason to worry. However, financial planning and how your work is distributed upon your death has bearing, and many successful artists do spend time setting up foundations and doing estate planning. Also, if you are that successful, then perhaps you have the financial strength to also consider some of the strategies that are discussed in this book-- for example, establishing your own entity to preserve your work and reputation and establishing permanent exhibition space, rather than having to rely on dealers to distribute your works to museums and outside organizations.

I am assuming that many of you have had, so far and hopefully will continue to have, a respectable career consisting of dozens of group and one-person exhibitions, having had your work sold to various collectors and enthusiastic owners or businesses, with a few works in museums and/or prominent collections, and perhaps a number of critical commentaries about your work that were printed in catalogs, newspapers and art magazines. In today's world, if you started straight out of school, you could be an art 'veteran' with 20 to 30 years under your belt, and still not be a member of AARP.

For those who haven't quite achieved this status, however, this book is equally relevant because it means that you are probably still striving to gain recognition. Strategies that I'll be describing might be your answer!

But as one continues to work and continues to mature, you should keep an eye to what will eventually happen. As you decide on where to live and work, what type of studio to get and under what conditions, you should keep your ultimate goals in mind.

WHO CARES?

To begin with, I am assuming that the artist cares. The artist dedicates a lot of time to each work, and to a career. After decades of work, it's not fair to treat artwork so casually. There are artists who will say, "When I'm dead, burn it all." They don't really mean it; what they are really saying is that they don't know what to do and can't make the effort to figure it out. Because there's no apparent demand for their work, it will just be a depressing task, and therefore to be avoided. Most artists would rather keep their heads in the sand.

In reality, unfortunately, few people care; we all live in fairly small social circles. Even for the most famous of names, history is for those who care about the subject matter. There are a few, in fact just a handful of names that enter the general population's vocabulary - Michelangelo, Di Vinci, Van Gogh, Picasso. That's pretty much the list for most of the western world (keep in mind that in the United States, 80% of high school students can not locate the city of Chicago on a map). If people have a better education, then you could add a dozen or more names, such as Raphael, Rubens, Monet, Braque, Mondrian, Pollack, Warhol. Recently, Campbell's Soups wanted to commemorate the 50th anniversary of Warhol's soup paintings, so they made four Warhol-style soup can designs, selling them through Target stores at the regular 75-cent price. I picked up a few for fun, and noticed some adults not understanding who Warhol was. The point is that only a very sophisticated audience knows the lineup of the art stars. Obviously, it's a big world, so that audience is quite large and that's why auction values hold up over time. But for the majority of artists, which must be 99.99% of us, we will be more or less forgotten about after a few years or a few decades. Certainly in 100 years, some of us might be at best footnotes, of interest only to a few scholars.

The art world is an exciting sphere of activity because we are participating in it. Step back a few steps and you can begin to see it in perspective, and how it stacks up with other interests, concerns and issues that every person in the world has on his or her mind.

In the same sense, art that has been sold for major installations in office building lobbies, for example, or for a new shopping mall complex, will only be a part of that complex as long as the owners want it to be there. At some point, buildings get razed as they have served their function, and new ones go up in their place. Even more common, buildings get renovated, from top to bottom; out goes the old wall covering, the old heating and air equipment, the old windows, the old flooring, the old furniture and reception desks, and the old "art." That has happened to me, and although a work of art might have sold for thousands of dollars years earlier, in the process of doing a $20 million makeover (and often many times that), it often costs the contractors more money to deal with something rather than putting it into a dumpster. I've seen "almost new" furnaces, couches, lights and art go into the dumpster by workmen who really don't care except to expedite their removal.

That's the sober reality, but if you are a fan of art, either as a practitioner or as a collector or just as an enthusiastic viewer, the world of art is important and one that should be treasured. That means all quality art, not just the art that has been popularly accepted or that the museums have anointed for their galleries.

WHO DESERVES TO START AND RUN AN ART MUSEUM?

Museums are large enterprises, usually involving millions of dollars in private funding and getting equal amounts through grants, endowments, government support, tax credits, and so forth. They are, what most artists regard as, the establishment. Artists are outside that arena, unless we think about the few art-superstars or the very infrequent inclusion in a museum's group show.

So museums seem to most artists to be big powerhouses, not much different than what General Electric or Ford are to the world of corporations. Let me state that you need to get that idea out of your heads! Museums can come in all sizes and configurations. They can be open daily or open on a few nights or a season. They can contain thousands of square feet like the Metropolitan or Louvre, or they can be as tiny as a single bedroom. Size needs not be the criteria. Basically, if you were famous and you dropped dead tonight, your studio could become a national treasure and be open to the public. The pertinent question is, would anyone come?

If you think people would come just because of your name, then you should have no problem. But there are other reasons for people to visit a museum. Obviously, if the quality of the art is high, then its reputation would encourage art lovers to visit. If the museum/attraction were in a tourist location, then people might just drop in if it were convenient. If the exhibition were free, there would be an extra incentive. If the exhibition were connected to another reason to visit, then that might help. For example, if it were part of a lobby or part of a restaurant or specialty store, people would come anyway and the exhibition portion might be the bonus.

But the fact that it might be about one artist should not, in itself, be the deterrent. If your name were Warhol, O'Keeffe, Rauschenberg, or Kahlo, no one would blink an eye upon hearing that there was going to be a museum for that one artist (and many famous artists around the world do have public museum/studios). So why should you doubt that you deserve a museum in your honor? Obviously, only because you are not a household name. Let me state again, that shouldn't rule it out. Why wait until the establishment chooses to include you? If your work is good, it should be seen. If you die, is that reason for your work to no longer be on view?

To expand this discussion some, let's think about collectors. They might have a valuable group of art works, both in monetary value and in artistic value. But it might not be suited for the MoMA or the Metropolitan. Should the works be distributed upon the owner's death? Often the collection as a whole represents a curator's eye, a relationship among the works that would be lost if separated. If the owner wanted to keep the collection intact, then the choice is to either donate it to a larger entity with that proviso, or to set up an entity- i.e. a museum - so the collection will be seen as a collection. Does that take millions of dollars to achieve? It can, but it can also be done for a lot less.

If an artist's work is part of the collection, then one aspect of the artist's work will remain in the public eye. Taking this one step further, if an artist is good enough to be in a museum collection, why not as a solo museum?

At first blush, this thinking can be seen as a big ego trip. But if the art is good enough for various collections, why not expand that idea? I'd like to get rid of this whole notion of ego-- yes, artists have egos-- if they didn't, I doubt they'd be so dedicated to making new art. You need an ego to think you can create something new and exciting, that you can push art to new grounds, that your art will deserve public viewing and be purchased, that your art is worth preserving rather than it being an exercise made for the trash. The art world is full of egos- I doubt anyone will contradict that statement.

The real question, is the quality of the art good enough so that it can stand on its own among its competition in other contemporary art museums and be worthy of public viewing now and in ten years and in a hundred years?

YOUR OWN GOVERNMENT HISTORICAL MARKER

During my own development, I've also dealt with issues of who gets recognized and who doesn't, and of course, probably because I was the struggling artist looking for recognition (which brings many more opportunities to make great works of art than remaining obscure), perhaps I was jealous about not having been plucked out and elevated. In any case, many years ago when still living in Washington D.C., I came up with this fun conceptual project, where I wrote and designed the "Historical American Artists Series." These were descriptions meant to be inscribed onto bronze plaques, where I said that "Eric Rudd, born such and such, lived or worked in this place" and then I gave a description. The idea was that if I were George Washington or someone famous, there would be an historical marker saying that I lived there as a boy, or worked there, etc. My plan was to execute this project if I had a major show again in a Washington gallery or museum - but I never did (as I write this). My plan was to mount these brass plaques onto heavy large stones (I can get limestone boulders inexpensively near my current studio) and put them on a truck with a lift, the type that lifts motors into and out of cars, and then early in the morning, drive around to the 15 or so designated places in the Washington D.C. area and quickly place a large stone with marker in front of where I lived, went to art school, had a first, second, third studio, and so forth. I also thought of having a DC lawyer ready to defend my rights, assuming I might be found and arrested for trespassing, vandalizing, endangering or littering. In some cases, I'm sure people would come out and assume the U.S. government had placed the marker and not know what to do about it. Either as a joke or an art happening, but I still like that idea. We'll see if I ever get a chance to do it. I think I've written most of the markers for the Washington area, which is where it's really meant to be since there are so many other historical markers there.

This is just a fun project for me, and one that I'll probably never do. The idea is that there are other ways to put your art 'out there' or to certify that your art is "worthy." I don't think artists have to wait for the establishment to give them the title of "worthy artist." Artists need to believe in themselves. You might spend money on a film and put it on YouTube. You might publish a catalog of your work and send it to all your friends and associates. You might have one grand last exhibition and then spend your time on simply distributing all your works. You can do all kinds of things if you aren't up to the task of permanently preserving your work.

Group Museum Venues for Artists

COMMUNAL WORK SPACE

Many years ago, I wanted a studio in the country so I could not only have a place to which I might escape, but also a place more conducive to building outdoor sculptures and do other types of work of which my city studio was less supportive. In the same way in which David Smith needed his Bolton Landing farm because his large-scale sculptures could not have easily been constructed in a New York loft space, I needed outdoor space as well.

Not being able to afford a nice country farm, I talked to some artists about going in with me in some sort of joint venture. I wanted to avoid a commune setting and all the personality issues that might evolve, but at the same time, I wanted to utilize the buying power that a small group of artists-investors-users might have. One concept was to look for a large farm with a main house and several guest cottages. Each owner would have one cottage and the main house could be divided into studios and eating facilities. Hopefully there would be a large barn or two for serious workspace. We would hire a caretaker couple to maintain the place and even cook meals. So if I were going to visit, for example, I could call ahead and my dinner would be awaiting me in the main dining room, assuming I wanted to share a meal with whoever was there at the same time. The chances were that even if several artists shared the property, most likely not more than two would be there at any one time. This was to be used as a secondary studio/escape; and in any case, the cottages would have kitchenettes if I chose to eat privately. This way, each artist could live as though we had money but in reality, it could be quite affordable. Such a venture might have evolved into an artist colony, where visiting artists and general visitors could have come and even stayed. This might have also become an alternative exhibition space someday. While I found a few artists who had interest in pursuing the concept, nothing materialized, perhaps because I never found the perfect property. But the idea stayed with me - that the value of joint investment could pay off if one could prevent personality conflicts from tearing the goals apart.

Remember, group activities are fraught with pitfalls.

This idea continues to be the most logical solution for projects involving large physical space Buying "large" is the only way to get the price per square foot down to downright "cheap." So if three, five, ten or more artists could ever have the foresight, they could pioneer incredible alternative art spaces – for studio, for residential and for exhibition – both while the artists are alive and for continuing exhibition after the artists are gone.

THE HEAVIES

Artists usually don't care much about institutions—museums and such seem to have a life of their own, far removed from the everyday struggles of the artist. Many artists will have some interaction with big museums, such as having a work included in a show or in their collection, but generally few artists are really involved with how a museum operates.

Traditionally, most museums have evolved from palaces or grand collections. I grew up in Washington D.C. where the heavies included the National Gallery of Art, which became the nation's main art museum, fueled by the Mellon Collection. The other main heavy was the Corcoran. But during the 60s, contemporary art, which had been poorly relegated to basements of various government buildings, found light in new homes-- which are now the National Portrait Gallery and the Smithsonian American Art Museum. Subsequently, President Johnson made a deal and built the Hirshhorn Museum after the Joseph H. Hirshhorn's collection was offered to the government. But the city's jewel was really a small museum, the Philips Collection. In rooms of this small mansion filled mostly by Impressionist and early abstract art works. I spent quite a few hours as a student admiring Klee, Kokoschka, many Impressionists, the Rothko room, and more.

Moving to the Berkshires in 1990, I found here the counterpart to the Washington D.C. Philips Collection in the Clark Art Institute, built as a country residence by Sterling and Francine Clark to protect their art collection should New York be attacked (during World War II). The residence was designed with the intention that it would be a museum open to the public. This museum has now expanded and is considered the "Getty - East Coast." More important to my interest and what was especially revealing to me was the brainstorm that Tom Krens (who later became the Guggenheim director) had to begin a new art museum in 800,000 square feet of abandoned mill-factory space. The project took fourteen years to get off the ground, but it finally opened in 1999 as MASS MoCA.

The Massachusetts Museum of Contemporary Art (MASS MoCA) in North Adams, MA; one of the largest art museums in the country, with room to expand. (photo by Kelly Lee)

I find many museums are beginning to have the same variety of art, with one work by each of the big mainstream names, while collections can have a unique point of view, and therefore retain a certain character that is worth preserving - at the same time keeping the collection intact. But the museums in the Berkshires have a distinct character, either because of the special collection each museum represents, or in the case of MASS MoCA, because it's such a big space in renovated mill buildings which allows it to show large art that many museums can't display simply due to size limitations. The original idea behind MASS MoCA was that the huge museum could have 5, 10 or 15 works by the same artist, and they could accommodate large works, on view for longer periods, that were too big for traditional museums. Without a permanent collection, MASS MoCA could concentrate on showing new art.

Art museum space is about real estate. If there exists a palace and some art and lots of money, a country or state or group can create a museum. If someone has a fabulous collection, a governmental body might chip in enough to build the museum. But in either case, substantial amounts of wall and floor space are the necessary components for displaying the art. If you have large space, you can put more on display. If you have smaller space, you either show fewer works or show smaller works. Museo Vedova in Venice, Italy is the former studio of the late Emilio Vedova. Designed by the architect Renzo Piano (who also designed the Menil Collection in Houston), due to its limited space, some of the paintings are viewed on moving conveyor belts. It is another exciting example of a smaller single-artist museum.

There are many variations on showing art. A step below what a well-financed museum might do, are many options that are still viable but much more affordable. Not all "new" or "artist" museums have to compete with the Guggenheim, MoMA or Whitney.

BIG SPACES FOR SALE CHEAP

When I started searching for big spaces, I kept touring industrial buildings. All over New England and the industrial belt of the United States, manufacturing was dying. Factory and mill buildings were almost being given away. However, a big building that needs a new roof, new windows, a new heating system, a new electrical system, and perhaps worst of all, a hazardous waste cleanup, can be a nightmare not even worthy of consideration. Nonetheless, out of the thousands of buildings, there were dozens if not hundreds of buildings that had fewer of these problems.

The other factor is location, not just in which region, but which area within a town. A place that has no connection to the arts might still be acceptable if all efforts will then go toward stimulating culture in that place. It won't work if no one has any interest in introducing culture to the area. And then, if you decide it is a good region or city or town, is the specific location easy to get to? Is it sandwiched between other industries that would not be compatible for an arts center or museum? When I moved to the Berkshires, I had the best of both worlds - cheap and abundant space existing in a very cultural environment. But I had previously toured and rejected countless buildings that had no chance of being transformed to an arts space.

Mill buildings are still available, although they are getting fewer in number as one of two things have happened to the many available buildings over the past two decades. Either they have finally been purchased and renovated for some reuse, or they have not been purchased in which case they have most likely received little to zero maintenance, and are now in a condition such that they are not economically salvageable. Adding to the strain is the fact that building codes have become much stricter and costs of building materials and labor have gone sky high, increasing renovation costs greatly.

Nevertheless, take a look at the numbers. I've purchased mill space for less than one dollar per square foot. Now rental rates in most areas of the country are several dollars a foot per year, so when I talk about a dollar a foot for purchase, that's a fraction of what it costs for normal real estate. If you are a bit vague about this subject matter, do read, The Art Studio/Loft Manual-- it tells you all you need to know about the ins and outs of real estate-- an essential subject in which all artists need to be well versed.

In my area, which is typical of many areas throughout the United States, churches have declining membership and many are being sold. I just purchased my second church at a bargain rate - about five dollars a foot, but that's still what a normal rental would be for a year, and this was for a purchase.

Other areas of the country will have their own bargains. For example, another national trend is the re-use of big box stores. Walmart, for example, often will build a big store, and then a few years later, will build a super Walmart nearby, discarding the older building. In our area, that's in process, and the existing Walmart store is for sale at the asking price of $1.2 million for 100,000 plus square feet.

This is a typical Walmart; this one happens to be for sale, as a new Super Walmart is soon opening nearby. Why not turn this into a perfect art center for artists?

Now I know, you are thinking that's a lot of money. But take a careful look. Pretend that it can be purchased for $1 million, and 20 artists get together for a joint studio and exhibition space. That's $50,000 for 1/20 of the space, which is 5,000 square feet. See what kind of space $50,000 will buy you in New York, Los Angeles, Chicago or Boston. Maybe a closet if you are lucky.

All of a sudden, this is not such an outrageous price - cheap enough so that if this is financed, and maintenance money is even thrown in, it could be as low as $300 or $400 a month per artist. Thinking about the Walmart in my town, this could be a summer studio for New York or Boston artists, which wouldn't require any of them to make life-changing commitments. If the project grew and took on momentum, then perhaps for those artists who got into the deal as founders, it could turn into a permanent museum space after they are gone.

In one specific case, I think a Walmart building can be purchased for even less money - perhaps well under $1 million for a newish building with high ceilings, asphalt parking for hundreds of cars (and outdoor sculptures), bathrooms, etc. By adding some partitions, artists could turn a building of that sort into a vibrant arts center. All of a sudden, one can apply some of my business models to allow for areas for studio work (the public can see ongoing art work being created), storage, exhibition space, and perhaps space that would focus on permanent storage and display after the artist's death.

The one in my town is one mile directly down the road from MASS MoCA. It would not take much to link it up with other art spaces in town, and the combined art spaces would create a critical mass that would take on a power of its own. But that's just here-- there are these types of opportunities all across the nation, and partnerships with new spaces that are reinventing the big box store castaways can be made with area colleges and other schools or cultural centers. This goes for performance spaces as well as for possible homes for various collections.

Who knows – discarded big box stores might be the future look of the typical 'artist' studio.

GROUP VENUES; SEEKING HELP AND SUPPORT FROM PEERS

I've talked about artist communities. There are virtual artist communities and that is a fairly new phenomenon. I'm a big believer in the Internet and email communication. I'm not yet into a Facebook presence. Perhaps I'll change; after all, just to get the word out about this book, using Facebook is the best way today.

Social media is a new buzzword, but for a reason. In my younger days, the artist community was small and we often had physical gatherings. As Washington D.C. grew and grew, hundreds of artists moved in or simply matured and became part of the art scene. Meanwhile, most of the 'original' core group of artists married, had children, attended the openings and parties less frequently, and moved about and farther away from each other.

Everyone has his or her own small circle of artist friends, but even as the art scene exploded in overall population, in some ways, the structures that stimulated artists to gather and work together on issues, broke down.

Social media has brought back a new type of closeness. My caution is that this media is for communication but has limited effect on the actual work. I know that some artists are using digital technology as their primary work, so that distribution over the Internet is the same as any other type of display. However, for the overwhelming majority of artists who make physical objects in an original media, distributing images of the work in web sites, for example, even if accompanied by explanations and discussions, is not the same as exhibiting the actual work in a gallery or museum where viewers can see the actual work.

Having said that, social media is a way of keeping in touch with fellow artists. The interesting point is that participants can be ageless. That is, a 'senior' artist can join a discussion with artists in their 20s, and none are the wiser. It allows for that one aspect to become a non-issue and a way that older artists can feel like they are part of the art scene.

ATTENDANCE

Big city museum have attendance figures that range under, or even exceed, a million visitors (Guggenheim, MoMA, LA County Museum). The new contemporary art museum in our town, MASS MoCA, has over 100,000 visitors annually. Nearby, the Clark Art Institute which shows Impressionist, early American and early European art, has had (depending on their big summer exhibition) upwards to 200,000 visitors. About an hour south, the Norman Rockwell Museum gets similar attendance. However, a house-studio turned summer museum, the Frelinghuysen Morris House and Studio gets only 2,500 visitors in guided tours during their summer and fall season.

Where would a single artist museum, perhaps unknown in the popular culture, fit among these numbers?

WELCOME TO THE VILLAGE OF MUSEUMS

If you are stimulated to think about your own exhibition space and then upon your death, having a museum-type space that will preserve and exhibit your art, the big question is - where? Most artists gravitate to big cities, but with cities come big city prices and costs. Real estate in New York, Chicago, San Francisco, as examples, is so expensive that it is difficult to conceive of anyone following my suggestions for a reasonable amount.

However, keep in mind one thing-- this has always been the assumption, so perhaps that's the reason nothing has been tried. I want to not only suggest individual attempts, but also that many attempts be made within the same destination. It is hard to duplicate what Disney can do, with many attractions in one campus-park. But if a hundred individuals took action in the same area, they would produce the same critical mass. One just has to be realistic about where cheap real estate opportunities exist. Even if it's expensive, a city location could still be considered. If artists shared one exhibition space, and shared storage space, the art could be rotated monthly. Like a time-share, 1/12 of the cost might be within an artist's financial reach, if use of the space for one month of the year is an acceptable allowance.

I matured in Washington D.C. where real estate was never easy but I found bargains. When you buy something for $50,000, or even later for $150,000, and twenty years later it's worth $500,000, how do you think a young artist will think about you? That young person might think you are a rich millionaire- wondering how you had the resources to own a building worth half a million dollars! Buy cheap, cover your costs, keep it a long time, be in an appreciating neighborhood, and you'll eventually own a valuable property which you can put to good use for your art purposes. And you'll own it outright because the mortgage will be fully paid off. Where to start? If it's too late for Washington D.C. or any major city, then look elsewhere.

OK, if you think buying property wherever you are is the equivalent of trying to buy property in Beverly Hills or Madison Avenue, let's explore alternatives. Donald Judd purchased an army base in Marfa, Texas. Others have gone to the desert in the southwest to install large environmental works. And I now live in a small town that is super cheap but happens to be in one of the best cultural spots in the nation.

There are alternatives. Perhaps visitors will be fewer the farther you venture from a major art city, but if you carry out your ideas as well as Judd did in Marfa, then the reputation will attract serious art viewers. Marfa isn't an easy trek for the casual visitor-- you have to make a real effort to go there. It's two or three hours away from any major airport so they only get several thousand visitors a year- but these are the visitors they and likewise you, want. These are people who really want to see the art and don't act like they walked into an art museum by mistake when they'd rather be in Madame Tussaud's Wax Museum.

Now let's continue with my example, using North Adams as a model. I envision not just one or two museums here, but perhaps 20 or 30 museums, permanent alternative spaces, and non-traditional galleries. Imagine all these entities within one 'theme park' campus.

MASS MoCA is the mother lode - the equivalent to the big roller-coaster ride at an amusement park, and second in line, if all goes well, the Rudd Art Museum will have three locations and might be one of the largest individual artist museums in the nation. In addition to that, there could be lots of other museum and alternative art spaces open to the public-- all part of a cultural theme park.

There are large mill spaces still available at bargain prices-- perhaps a group of collectors or artists could go in together to make one a museum and storage facility. There are scores of small stores, all centrally located and within a couple blocks from MoCA that could be purchased and turned into gallery-sized museum spaces. Maybe an installation artist would like permanent space for work that might be changed annually or not at all (think about The Broken Kilometer piece in New York). Art galleries are of course welcome to join the party, but I'm thinking of new types of alternative spaces that would have the feel of something unique and innovative. I'm also advocating for senior artists to present their very best in a carefully curated way, whether it is permanent or semi-permanent. There also happens to be cheap residential property and large churches, all for sale and all which could be transformed into art venues.

If even some of my suggestions come true, there could easily be thirty art spaces in town. Hopefully, visitors would come not only to go to MASS MoCA, but in the way people travel to Kassel, Germany every four years and spend a few days at Documenta, they would spend a few days making the rounds to all the spaces in the town (it would take that much time to cover all the exhibitions). This would take cooperation between the various venues, but the critical mass could attract far more visitors than any single venue could on its own.

The idea for creating a museum that would become a destination attraction, which would lure people interested in contemporary art to come to North Adams, Massachusetts, was the brainchild of Thomas Krens who later became the director of the Guggenheim Museum. In a way similar to that in which people are drawn to travel to Disneyworld or Disneyland by its uniqueness and its reputation, people really interested in contemporary art would feel compelled to travel to North Adams to see the "must see" art museum. People go to museums in large cities because they are there anyway for other reasons. They do not normally travel to a city specifically to experience a museum show. But for Disney parks, people travel specifically to go to the park--- that's their main reason.

So in our small town of North Adams, Massachusetts, three hours by car north from New York City and two and half hours west from Boston, people come to the Berkshires for a mix of recreation/country scenes and cultural offerings, which include three major art museums. If we had more, and our "cultural park" grew larger and larger with more and art offerings, the critical mass might make it attractive for more visitors. Rising seas raise all boats, as they say.

That's why I believe that smaller venues - namely mini-museums staged by artists - could ride on the coattails of the larger museums that have already proved their worth.

My wife and I drove across the country two times, trying to stay off of the interstates in favor of the secondary roads that took us through countless small towns and cities. So many had common problems, where the downtowns were almost empty except for some private and governmental activity during the day, and barely a sole around at night. Located a mile or two outside of the downtown centers would be the Walmarts, bowling alleys, movie theater complexes, motels, chain restaurants, big-box and chain stores, the malls, and so forth. All that downtown real estate going to waste! What did I see? Opportunities at low to bargain (to give-away) prices!

Building codes can be lethal when considering renovating old buildings, but a careful plan can make a project worthwhile. Someday, these towns will need to be revived. They are not going to be bulldozed. So why not let the artists pioneer their revival? In many cases, and this would be a new experience for most artists, the cities would roll out their red carpet to welcome the artists.

Many places are far from major cultural capitals and so that's a real negative consideration. Many do not have the sophisticated audience built in. But for all the negatives, I keep going back to one theme-- if it's that good and that unique, people will hear about it and people will come. It has to be on a scale that makes an impact. It has to be promoted so people have a way to know about it. But with the right mix of quality and energy, something special can occur.

It's like the Wild West, when land was free and people chased after it. Here, I think opportunity is being overlooked for one main reason. Artists want instant gratification and do not look at the long-term benefits. Artists should care more about making incredibly good art, and having it properly displayed. If more and more do this, and artists can achieve critical mass, then it really doesn't matter where it is. After all, it's pretty hard to get more distant than Marfa, Texas, and that is one great example of it being done right!

ANOTHER LARGE VENUE IDEA

Perhaps you know someone to whom you can pass on this book. This particular section is geared for that odd collector, entrepreneur or rich artist who is interested in a large project. This can lose money, can break-even and be organized as a non-profit project, or it could be tried for profit.

Typically, when thinking about museum-type space, one thinks about huge open space. Instead, pretend you find a small office building that is cheap. Now keep in mind, I've seen multi-million dollar buildings sold under bank foreclosure for a fraction of their worth during better economic times. Now pretend this building has a glass window façade, and four to ten offices per floor, and let's say it's six stories high-- so not necessarily a huge building.

Now lets pretend that my art sponsor/developer purchases this building and decides to turn it into an art display building, not too different from themed centers where dozens of similar type businesses gather within one complex. Instead of offices, the new owner selects different artists to make permanent (or semi-permanent) displays of their work; perhaps some works are installed minimally in sterile white cubes and other artists completely re-do the offices to make environmental installations.

Could this alternative art space become a hit? A typical office building is not the structure that an artist would first choose for an art museum, but what's available and cheap can always become a new trend. I can envision small office spaces becoming tranquil, meditative type spaces for more intimate work. Or I can envision an office suite being turned into a walk-through art installation. Certainly multi-media art can work well within smaller spaces.

And what other types of buildings can be used? If the zoning permits, could old apartment buildings be used, after the kitchens have been removed? If codes permitted, perhaps the structure could be left intact and only the walls could be re-skinned.

As you can tell, I'm interested in imaginative re-uses of obsolete or undervalued buildings, in a variety of settings. The re-use should involve a new way of presenting art to the public. The structure should stimulate artists to re-think what they want to make and how they want their art to be viewed.

In North Adams, there could be a stampede for cheap, run-down houses. All an artist needs is a working bathroom, a kitchenette and a place for a bed. The rest can be studio and exhibition space. Perhaps we'll have to change some zoning codes (that's easily done; we're a small town and very supportive of the arts) and we could have studios-residences-galleries scattered in a residential area that might also become an 'arts district.'

No one wants mobs of people roaming about a residential area than going to the commercial district, but open-studios or open-house art tours held twice a year or on summer weekends are probably an acceptable amount of traffic. This would mean visitation in the hundreds, not thousands, but that might be enough. Couple this with joint publicity through print and Internet, and this could be an attractive "second studio" for a New York or Boston artist, especially if there were mortgages made especially available for artists. Houses can be purchased for $40,000 (thereabouts), so their re-use would not require a huge investment. If I were the mayor, I'd line up not only financing, but also special funding or grants to make sure that the exteriors are fixed up. That would be a requirement for the property's use.

If 20 or 30 or 50 artists invested here to make this happen, the result could be a cultural statement that could have historical significance, and at the same time might just become successful in stimulating increased visitation to North Adams. And if this were then done in a few towns in each state, this country would be witnessing a whole new trend- and a positive one at that.

I mention North Adams because I live here and not because I'm trying to sell real estate to you. I only use it as an example. I have seen these types of bargains all across the United States, in the east, south, southwest, west, and Midwest. There are a lot of underutilized properties that can be yours for the asking.

The one nice aspect about artists and real estate is that we never kick other people out; we can't afford to. We go into neglected and cheap properties and end up bringing life back to a neighborhood or district or town. Just make sure you have ownership, so when the properties appreciate, you aren't the one being kicked out.

I'VE STARTED

How am I dealing with this? I still believe that real estate forms the foundation of your ability to do work, as well as to preserve your work. To help matters, there are bargains all over the United States. Even today, twelve years after I wrote about the bargains where I live in North Adams, a town that is in a culturally rich region, and fourteen years after MASS MoCA opened to the public, bargains continue to be available. I've just purchased a third building of 20,000 square feet - a magnificent stone church right in the middle of North Adams - and part of this church will become museum space for what I hope to carry out as a 3-building art museum for my art. The way it's evolving, my future museum could be the largest museum in the United States devoted to a single artist.

I don't have the cash that the project really needs, but I'm hoping that part of the real estate can be rented in perpetuity and will support the portion that will be used for museum exhibitions. It's a dream and one that I've been building towards for many years.

My initial emphasis was to have affordable studio space, but as I've gotten older, I've spent more time in thinking about how to set up permanency. We'll see if my vision is realized. I don't want this to fizzle the way the Contemporary Artists Center fizzled under different leadership, after I stepped down as director.

It's an uphill battle when even the most detailed of wills/plans backed by loads of money can't be realized in perpetuity in most cases. For example, the Barnes Collection was so specific in stipulating that the paintings couldn't be changed from the exact places where they hung on the walls. Well, years later and with its share of mismanagement perhaps, the Barnes Collection is now a new museum-- not as intended by Mr. Barnes. He would be turning over in his grave. So without the endowment of millions, I face a formidable battle ahead, but so far, I've accomplished a lot and hope I can continue. It's not fair to dump onto my children more art than most major art museums have. They would not be able to deal with it. There are more horror stories out there with which I don't want to scare you. Let me just summarize with this - most art, truth-be-told, ends up in attics, basements, flea markets and dumpsters. If your art is credible, then you'll have to put time and effort and creative intelligence into preserving your life's work.

MORE ABOUT REAL ESTATE

Over and over again, I've stressed how important real estate is, especially to establishing a working studio where you can realize your dreams, without compromise.

To summarize a few points: I've traveled all over the world and all over the country and I've come to understand a few principles.

a. *Big cities are frightfully expensive. Unless you have oodles of money, you'll not be able to carry out ambitious plans in prime territory of New York, Chicago, Los Angeles, Miami, and other major centers.*
b. *All over the country, and some cases not that far away from major*

cities, are rural lands, small towns and medium cities that are all in need of economic recovery, and where real estate is available - reasonably to very inexpensively.

c. *In medium-sized cities, where the main commercial stores and centers (box stores, movie complexes, bowling alleys, motels, etc.) have moved to the outskirts - into new commercial strip-malls, the downtowns are distressed and begging for buyers and tenants.*

d. *National trends have made additional types of real estate available for bargain prices. Churches are downsizing, big box stores are expanding into newer/bigger box stores and jettisoning their old stores, and depending on the region, certain industries are in a downturn; these can include motels, single movie theaters, factories, mills, etc.*

e. *Anyone with any budget, willing to travel a bit, can afford the real estate that's out there. Anyone! But you have to be brave and daring.*

These truths I know. So I can tell you with confidence that I can go to hundreds of locations and readily find a bargain space. What I can't tell you, unless I spend a few days, is whether there is a rationale for an arts center to be in that town. Specifically, does it make sense for a specific town to be host to a cultural attraction, like a single-artist museum?

What reason should the town want one? Well, perhaps there is a small college in the area that has an art department and so it might create a synergy for the art department to partner with your art proposal. Perhaps there is a theater or other cultural facility in the town, so that an additional one gives the town some critical mass. Perhaps there is a natural or historical attraction in the town that draws visitors anyway, and perhaps your art museum idea will give tourists something else to do, especially on a rainy day (museums love the rain!). Perhaps there are other vacant buildings, and in the same way that MASS MoCA drew lots of attention and support as a major economic development project in North Adams, on a smaller scale, your proposal will draw all the support and attention, and it will then lead to others following in your footsteps. Maybe an arts-based economy can become the town's master plan and salvation.

Perhaps you can link up with an unlikely partner. If there's a special inn, restaurant, historic site, or some commercial enterprise that you think will survive another few generations and be there in a 100 years, then being geographically close or somehow linked can keep your art venue thriving.

Whatever the connection, you should be able to forge some partnership. If not, perhaps there is no reason to locate there and you should look elsewhere. On the other hand, if the facility will be so different, so strong and so alluring, then you can always hope that people will make the pilgrimage to your art project no matter what the distance from another cultural site or public transportation.

And for my region, where I know almost every building, I can report that despite the presence of two respected colleges, three nationally known art museums, and various other cultural organizations, real estate is still affordable.

I keep thinking, what's the matter with everyone? What will it take? I guess I'm hoping that this book, and my previous books, will reach a few more artists who will see the light.

But I'm not trying to pull you here, to North Adams. Instead, I really want to drive across the country again, and find these kinds of alternative art museums in town after town, city after city, all across the nation. I want the state and federal arts agencies to support these efforts. I want new energy to go to downtowns that are looking worn and tired. I want artists to stop making saleable art that can fit into the trunks of cars, when their real masterpieces might be impractical and not saleable. I want to be surprised and astonished by a new trend in art, that's coming out of unlikely environs on an ambitious scale that surpasses what's being done in New York. I want people to do this when they are young and to do this when they are mature, and for all kinds of estate museums to be formed. I want nothing less than a revolution of sorts.

And to my mind, only because I'm doing it myself and I wasn't born with a silver spoon and I don't have the fame to just make this happen easily, I can state to you that if I can do it, then it's very, very possible for others to do it as well.

It's Really to Help You, The Artist

TO MAKE THE BETTER ART

If an artist were offered a choice of two shows-- one in the "Projects" room at the Museum of Modern Art in New York, and the other at a reputable New York- Chelsea private art gallery, my bet is that the artist would choose the MoMA show. And my bet is that a typical show at a New York gallery would be comprised of, let's say for argument sake, medium to large paintings, but ones that are easily transported and can be sold to collectors to hang in their New York apartments. The show at MoMA however, would probably be much different. This might be the opportunity for an artist to create something large, an installation or special work that is less 'salable.'

Now galleries have traditionally made exceptions. When I showed there early on, the shows in the Jefferson Place Gallery in Washington D.C. (which showed Ken Noland, Gene Davis, Sam Gilliam, and Anne Truitt, among others) often would host shows that were mini-museum shows. That was because the Corcoran, the only large museum at the time that occasionally showed DC artists, didn't show local artists with enough frequency, so on occasion, artists gave demonstrations of their museum-scaled shows at the Jefferson Place.

There have been quite a few ambitious gallery shows over the years. In New York, James Rosenquist installed his painting, F-111, all around the gallery room, as an installation. That large work is now in the collection of MoMA. But even though there are exceptions, galleries tend to want work that can sell easily, and so the tendency is for artists to scale their artwork appropriately.

The point I'm making is that sometimes artists need to push themselves to make the riskier art, the art they really want to make even if it might be less practical and result in less money. In crowded studios, without invitations from museums, how can artists go this route?

My answer is to give yourself the opportunity - to control how the work will be seen yourself rather than be beholden to a curator or museum director selecting you. And even if you do have an invitation once in a while, the exhibition will be for a few weeks - and then when will the next opportunity arise? If you had expansive space for this purpose, you could do what you wanted, when you wanted. As we get older, we think in terms of impact rather than just selling a few more works.

In 1977 I developed a large project using theme park technology. Although I made some attempts to realize my dream, I never had the money or resources or space to carry it out. However, as a result came one of those "moments" when I realized that I needed to secure space to do this work. The project was so large and complicated that I also realized that I needed permanent space for it. I couldn't build it quickly, and once installed, I didn't want to dismantle it after just a few weeks or months. Because of the connection of my project to theme parks, I also started thinking about how viewers experience a theme park ride, and how many might pay for this experience and under what circumstances. For my art-based ride idea, I expanded my thinking to allow for lay people, who might have little familiarity with formal art, to be interested in coming. Up until then, I just accepted the notion that normal gallery viewers were people with sufficient interest and knowledge about art. But I thought that there might be other ways to attract a broader audience, and then to get them to appreciate the art aspect.

All this led me to analyze the economic obstacles as well as opportunities. That was the beginning of my planning for a space where I could realize my vision and open it up to the public, and hopefully charge an admission fee. Rather than trying to sell my work, I was going to attempt a different economic plan and wanted to finance its operation with admission fees. This was a concept normally undertaken and executed by established museums or full-fledged amusement parks, not by a single artist with limited resources.

Admittedly, it took me 19 years to realize my vision. My quest led me searching for spaces all over the United States (it turned my travels into "business trips" because no matter where I was, I looked at unused and abandoned properties). Twelve years after this first thought, I had secured a 130,000 square foot mill building in a culturally rich region - for peanuts! But it took me another six years before I was in a position to carry out my project, which was finally built in 1995 and opened up to the public in 1996 as the "Dark Ride Project." It was a 15,000 square foot exhibition where the highlight was an 11-minute ride on a computer-controlled vehicle through my "art space." It was quite sensational, if I may say so. I operated it for ten years before changing the format. It never achieved the level of a Disney attraction, but it has led me in many new directions.

My main disappointment, other than that it never achieved national recognition in the major art publications, is that it was too ahead of where the town was; after all, MASS MoCA was still four years away from opening when the Dark Ride Project opened. I had a long-shot hope that it might generate enough attendance to pay for many types of upgrades and operational expenses. It was a mini-Disney park, in a sense, but with pure art as the main feature. A self-sustaining cultural facility is still a goal for me, but it might be as farfetched as building a 'machine that creates more energy than it uses.' As you know, most museums only cover part of their expenses through admission fees, the rest coming from donations and grants.

This type of project is not easy to carry out, nor is creating paintings that don't fit a normal wall above a couch. But no matter what ambitious project you want to carry out, an artist-controlled space might be the solution. My project didn't quite make it, and it would be harder for something like that to open without my personal attention, but the concept has potential. It needs to be fine-tuned.

Now I'm not advocating that you pick up your tools and bags and move somewhere to do this work. However, a reasonable first measure might be to find studio space outside of your major city (for those in big cities) and use that space as a weekend, summer or winter getaway studio. In the same way that famous artists have used their summer or country studios for special work, only to move there more or less full time in their senior years (Henry Moore comes to mind first), you can secure a place to carry out work that will later be a place where you can 'downsize' to (only in the sense that you might want to reduce your main studio or your city studio and residence, or downsize expenses as you trade up in size). Additionally, as you prepare for what will happen after you are gone, this new space could also become your permanent solution for storage and display space forever.

Donald Judd purchased some buildings and then later part of an army base in the boondocks of Texas. It is one of the premier examples of what a single artist can do. Go to Marfa, Texas and see for yourself. He had vision and ambition. Yes, he had a reputation and some assets that certainly made it easier than most, and he was joined by a few other invited artists. The Chinati Foundation now runs the various properties that dominate the tiny town, but the quality of the art and the fact that dedicated viewers go hours out of their way to experience it, is something that everyone needs to examine closely for inspiration.

HOW TO DO THIS WITH LIMITED RESOURCES

There are other examples and I urge you to look around your region. Later I will tell you how I came about establishing my own foundation for working and preserving my art. Do not let traditional thinking narrow your options. Take a walk, examine your life and see if you have overlooked some exciting ways to produce and preserve your art.

This is an ambitious undertaking and one that I would not expect the masses of artists to try, but it is one that a few of you might be ready to consider.

That's hard enough, but now here's the other hard part. Unless you get as lucky as I did in finding dirt-cheap beautiful space that won't bankrupt you with hazardous waste, roof, structural or other issues, this type of activity is not inexpensive. So what to do?

The obvious answer is to pool resources. The difficulty of that is, who do you know who is on the same wave-length as you, who has the resources to contribute his or her share, who has the staying power, the quality of art, the wherewithal to deal with the issues that will come up, the personality to deal with the community in a positive way, and the ambition to do something great?

Marriage is difficult enough; partnerships can be deadly. So while I'm bullish that it can be done, it's just not easy. I won't pretend to you that it is. Rarely is doing something that is "pushing the envelop" simple or easy. Plus, whenever you are "out there" on a limb, there are those (way too many from my experience) who have nothing better to do than take pot shots at you. But if your heart and soul is in the right place, and if your talent is being challenged, you can be successful.

MAKING IT HAPPEN

There are many possible partnerships. There are collectors who might be willing to fund an ambitious project. There are galleries that might be able to help as they use part of this an alternative show space for themselves. There are organizations that can help. You need to decide on the scope of what you are trying to do, and then determine the people around you, or who in theory, might have interest in the outcome.

Once you've narrowed your search, there are many possible sources for money or funding. For example, there might be an educational aspect that would be perfect for grants. What you are really doing is trying to establish an 'alternative art museum,' not much different from spaces that opened up across the United States a few decades ago. You can give it the same" establishment feel" by structuring it with a board and well-designed PR, or you can go into it alone.

Across the nation, there are 'burned out' towns needing revival. Artists have traditionally been the folks who have gone into bad neighborhoods and turned them around, only for the eateries and boutiques to move in as higher rents drive the artists out (except for those smart artists who purchased rather than rented their lofts).

Just the other day, I was contacted by someone representing a small town in Iowa, an hour or so west of Chicago, about trying to stimulate development in the town to attract artists. If the town has empty buildings, or ample land, all kinds of possibilities exist. Artists are considered marketable commodities, and you can use this cache to sell your ideas to a community. I'll mention other real estate ideas because, as you can begin to understand, a physical place is necessary for working purposes and hopefully to preserve your work. You can also read my other books for more details; I can't emphasize enough that you can be very ambitious if you really want to carry out large-scale, visionary projects.

What Others Have Done

WHAT OTHERS HAVE DONE

History is full of famous and not-so-famous cases of artists' estates being manipulated after the artist's death, usually for the monetary gain of someone who is in the driver's seat and has greedy motives.

My artist-historian friend, Charles Giuliano, talks about how Karl Knaths' work fell into his widow's hands. Since she lacked the ability to handle the estate, a bank took over her affairs, attempting to convert the art into income for her. The work was put into a bank vault, and the bank attempted to sell the art on its own. Needless to say, speculators got involved, purchased in bulk and managed to get tax credits out of donated work. As this process was going on, no one was there to look at it from the point of view of the artist - to maintain his reputation and to preserve the work intact. For example, the bank ransacked notebooks and ripped out drawings to try to sell them individually. Fire sales, as was discussed with the tax estate sale of the David Smith's sculptures, will send the market value into a free-fall.

The failure to have a foundation and a management system in place, allowed the work to be tossed about for quick gain for someone, but not for the benefit of Knath's widow and certainly not to protect the integrity of the artist's reputation. Unfortunately, this is too common.

Gallery directors and art experts, whom you would expect to appreciate the value of an artist's reputation, have time after time demonstrated a greed for immediate gain, and have raped an estate and even manipulated the work (again, in the case of David Smith when the paint was removed, or in destroying Knath's sketchbooks to make the drawings more saleable) just to squeeze a few more dollars out of the loot.

If there is no apparent market value, then this won't happen because no one will even bother to deal with the work. How can an artist expect greater fame after his or her death? The romance of being a poor artist during one's career but suddenly, upon death, being discovered and becoming world famous, the Vincent Van Gogh story for example, is more folklore than reality. Reputations can increase, but rarely will an artist go from pauper to king upon death.

At least in the case of painters and sculptors, there are physical objects that have a chance to go somewhere and to be preserved. In the case of conceptual and installation artists, whose work might only be a temporary experience, how do you preserve the work? Mostly by documentation, through writing, video, digital images, and so forth. But again, someone needs to spend time to assemble all the materials and put them together in some form of print or digital catalog. This is difficult even with the artist's active participation and almost impossible once the artist is out of the picture.

As a critic and historian, Charles Giuliano has been asked countless times to help artists whom he has befriended or written about, because artists want their work to be brought together into some sort of intelligent package in the form of a book, article or catalog. But how can he take something like that on without compensation? One could spend many months for a properly researched article, catalog or book, and for that, one needs to make a substantial investment - one that is rarely done. That's what curatorial departments of museums do for major shows, but that leaves out 99.9% of the art world.

Charles is even concerned that written content is not being properly archived. Content needs to be in a digital cloud, so that if a web site is not continued, the content won't be lost. In the case of his own web site, www.BerkshireFineArts.com, he has arranged for the web site to continue after his death for at least ten years. A reasonable effort such as that is an exception rather than the rule. How do we stimulate more of that to happen? He has also looked into donating his files to the Archives of American Art, but the indications are that they are overwhelmed with materials and vastly underfinanced. Just because materials are under one roof does not mean they will be used, or even properly available. University libraries might offer better options, but the materials have to make sense for their specialized interests, and also need to be funded with cash. Imagine someone receiving boxes upon boxes of materials; what incentive is there for someone to sift through the materials? The longer it takes to get papers placed and the longer it takes to use the material, the more easily it will be forgotten.

As Charles expressed, "these are sobering and daunting issues that creators face as we come to the end of long and productive careers."

The artist should have the most incentive to preserve his or her life's work, but when I visit most studios, I see artists barely keeping up with proper storage of current inventory. It's not surprising that artists don't spend additional efforts on the future. Usually, it's just dumped into someone else's lap.

Heirs repeatedly seek to unload art to museums, but directors will rarely take any on unless they deem the art worthy of the collection and unless the gift is accompanied by a sizeable cash donation or an escrow fund, to pay for the cost of storage, preservation and curatorial work. It's a big project to deal with so much work; at most, a museum might take a single work, subject to size. A relationship with a collector of your art, who is willing to take on an artist's estate, would be a glorious solution; but I do not know of any; I hope you do!

A good book to read interviews with people who have handled artists' estates is Artists' Estates by Magda Salvesen and Diane Cousineau.. Estates large and small are discussed and the realities, in most cases difficulties, are brought to light. Pay special attention to the smaller, lesser-known artists. In one or two cases, I knew something about the situation. Some estates have been temporarily saved by an executor or dealer in charge, but my fear is that once that person goes, the estate will go down the tubes. Although few artists will have the assets valued at the sums of the foundations most often mentioned, I believe that you can imitate their operations with a modest, scaled-down model. Some of the foundations mentioned have millions of dollars in assets, and receive tens if not hundreds of thousands of dollars in royalties from copyrights. I assume that will not be the case for most artists reading this book.

Artists' Estates is a fascinating read. It consists of mostly first-person interviews with folks who are dealing with artists' estates. Most are family members- spouses or children, and a few are trustees and executors of the larger foundations. The first person narratives will tell you the struggles, failures and successes that each have had. Most of the artists are familiar names; some not so big but are known enough so that their work has appreciated in value since their deaths. Without substantial assets and interest from museums and dealers, most would not easily survive. So for most artists, it is an uphill battle for sure, but one that I think can be mastered. This book is really the only one that gives as much information on the subject, outside of the conference publication, _A Visual Artist's Guide to Estates_. Other than these publications, I would turn to the many books about foundations and estates geared for anyone, not just artists.

To contrast all the failures, there are clear examples show how advance planning and/or having sufficient value in the estate allows for the proper preservation to be carried out. That is why we have some superb single-artist museums and single-artist installations in the United States. We also have some of the finest museums that started out as private collections.

The point is, these good examples can be followed and put into practice by individual artists with fewer dollars or resources. It will require time and effort and continued investment.

Most of my acquaintances, who someday will have to deal with their art because they have a large inventory, have done practically nothing about it. Those with families probably have some sort of basic will, leaving assets to spouse and then children, but with a couple of exceptions, I have not heard that any are dealing specifically with their art - who gets what, how the art will be distributed (or disposed of), and so forth. It's not a pleasant subject not only because it means dealing with issues of or around death, but also because everyone wants to imagine that their art is worth a lot and will be highly prized, when the reality is that art more often becomes "stuff" that takes up space and costs money to keep.

My sculptor friend, Bruce Beasley, has built up over the years an amazing studio property in Oakland, California. His place is the first Bart (metro) stop once you cross the bay from San Francisco. Stay on the train for a few more stops and you end up in the middle of Oakland near the Oakland Art Museum, a very impressive museum that focuses on Californian artists.

Bruce started with an abandoned factory building and a few other buildings back in the days when real estate was cheap. At the time, it was not the best neighborhood. Over the years, he was able to acquire some adjoining properties, built a house and now has several buildings and a sculpture garden on about two acres of land.

The new building on the grounds of Bruce Beasley's studio in Oakland, CA, which will someday become the Bruce Beasley Sculpture Center.

When I last visited him, there was an enormous new steel and glass building, complete with a rolling overhead bridge crane to move about his large and heavy steel and stone sculptures. Bruce has worked hard and has been fortunate to have had many commissions during his career, so much of his work is out there in the public realm. But he has retained a number of pieces.

The minute I saw this large sculpture building, I knew it had been designed a little too elegantly for just a functional workspace. Sure enough, it turns out that Bruce has been thinking and doing something about what will happen to his work once he's gone.

The general plan is that the property, with all the buildings and his sculptures, will become a satellite museum for the Oakland Art Museum and will be called the Bruce Beasley Sculpture Center. Bruce wanted the center to not only be a permanent repository for his own work but also wanted it to make a contribution to the field of sculpture by providing a venue for other sculptors to show as well, and additionally to serve as a residency and work space for invited artists.

At the time of my visit, there was no written, ironclad agreement between Bruce and the museum to operate this facility in the future. There was a letter of understanding as all the pieces were gradually being brought together. These agreements take time to work through. Ruling out an untimely death, there is time to allow for a careful process. The museum also needs time to assess how to best make use of new assets, and most likely, they are not ready to operate a new facility at the moment. I'm sure there are many details that need to be carefully considered. One such consideration would be whether the museum may ever sell any of the works, another, what changes might be allowed at some future date, and so forth. Advance planning also gives the institution time to ramp up other programs in order to take advantage of the donation. The danger, of course, is that directors and museum policies can change; until there is a signed written contract between the parties, it remains a work in progress.

Nevertheless, this is an exemplary exception to the norm of someone who invested early in getting ample studio space, then developed the studio space for his own work processes, and additionally has been able to transform it to something that will have a second life, as it preserves Bruce Beasley's work for the future. This has all been done by one individual artist, although there will be an institutional partner which will take it on after Bruce is gone.

A New Industry

Artists' Estate Professionals -
A NEW ART INDUSTRY FOR TOMORROW

Imagine that there are "artists' estate professionals" (AEPs) who pitch their services to you. An AEP will arrange to collect your art, store your art in a fully insured facility, have exhibition rights so your work can be displayed in such diverse places as New York City and Miami and North Adams; your work will be digitized in catalog format and also presented on a web site (hosted by the AEP's company with a link to a web site under your name); furthermore, the AEP will handle sales of any work that you deem acceptable to sell (maybe only to museums and institutional collectors). Furthermore, your work will be promoted both commercially and by soliciting graduate students who might be given a monetary incentive to pick your career to study. Not a bad deal.

The cost of this? Well, there'll be the basic plan - with minimum storage space and limitations on the size of any one work that needs to be handled - of $7,000 a year. Then there are the fees for extra services - additional space, larger pieces, more exhibitions, exhibiting in the premier space in New York City, and so forth. For the "gold package" services, perhaps it will cost the artist $15,000 to $20,000 per year - still not a bad deal overall.

Lets assume that the company gets 30 artists paying an average of $12,000 a year. That's $360,000 gross income a year. Lets say that number expands to include 60 artists (still a tiny number in my opinion), then the gross income is $720,000 a year.

Remember, this example is just my imagination; it could become a reality.

Or a slightly different version: Let's say that a young graduate from an arts management degree program wants to go into business. And let's say that this person will perform all the services just mentioned for $5,000 a year, plus fees for storage and exhibition space. A client list of just 10 artists' estates will give that young person a gross income of $50,000 a year. Not bad just out of college and in this economy.

Space in North Adams, for example, can be had for pennies. Even if exhibition space is rented in New York, there's no need to rent NYC space in order to store the works in the city. It would be far cheaper to make a monthly run with a small truck to remove the existing show and install the works just being driven in.

How do we insure that all this will happen according to the contract, if the artist is no longer alive? Quite basic. As with the case for many contractors, the AEP would need to be bonded. This insurance bond means that should the AEP fail to perform or quit or whatever, the insurance bond would pay for the expenses of finding a reputable replacement.

Need more insurance? Pretend that a major insurance company, or a major bank, or a major museum, or even the state government should underwrite this industry, in the same way that you feel safe putting your money in a bank account because the U.S. government guarantees the safety of your money. Not only would this give the entire industry the solid foundation it needs, it would then stimulate many tiers of services.

Pretend that for every $50,000 the AEP brings in, 20% goes to the parent company. The AEP is earning a respectable $40,000 and the firm is making $10,000 from each AEP. There could be 100 or more AEPs. And best of all, if the "firm" has an art connection, there's a better chance of more prestigious exhibitions. Perhaps a museum-firm would attract artists by offering special exhibition space under this program, and as a result, bring in $1,000,000 income. There would be some administrative expenses, but you get the idea-- the numbers can be adjusted to reflect the realities of the operation. Nevertheless, it would not be unreasonable to expect that thousands of baby-boomer artists would be attracted to retain these services.

Some AEP firms might offer tiered or "platinum" services based on artistic merit rather than being part of the paid service open to anyone. They might make certain exhibition spaces not guaranteed for anyone who is a client, but only for those clients' works that have been accepted for display by the curator. In other words, the works are protected, but the extent of exhibiting the works might be dependent on a gallery director's judgment.

Once one or two or five of these firms get off the ground, there could be a stampede of museums, arts management university programs, insurance companies -- who knows who else? They might form alliances with one another. The bottom line-- there's a lot of potential business out there that no one has mined. And I can tell you one thing - those entities could use additional income.

And if these services are then linked to services for artists while they are alive, such as storage, digitizing, archiving records and building up assets like an investment quality insurance policy-- then when the artist dies, the funds will be there. In a sense, these services should be offered to artists through a new type of AARP long-term insurance for artists. With a monthly fee, for example, of $250 a month, the artist would be entitled to the full services in case of sudden death. But if the same artist continues to pay over the rest of his or her lifetime, then he or she would still benefit from the full services upon death. Doing this via an insurance policy would be easier for most artists, but that would not rule out the firm accepting full payment from an artist upon death.

Obviously, there may be many, many varieties and ways this concept can be fine-tuned. Overall, I'm confident it can work. Whether anyone has the foresight to get it off the ground and prove its merit will remain to be seen.

This is an imaginary industry at the moment; if I ran an arts management program, I'd put this into action immediately. All this could easily happen tomorrow, or next year, or before you have to make a choice about your art.

GOVERNMENT, BANK AND INSURANCE ROLE

There are many governmental programs to help with low-income housing and urban development projects. Unfortunately, most of them are old fashioned for today's world, and almost totally ignoring the needs of a large arts community.

A state arts agency could become the guarantor of an artist's building, of an artist's warehouse, or of an artist's estate firm. A state's arts agency could also persuade a bank or insurance company to take the business lead in such a program.

I have a friend who in the 1980s worked for Met Life Insurance and pioneered the long-term care insurance policies that then took off throughout the nation. In those days, the concept was new; now it has become a standard.

The same should happen with government arts agencies. The principle is the same. One pays into a policy and like most insurance, if you need it immediately, you get the benefits. If you don't, you continue to pay a reasonable fee until you do need it, if ever. There are devils in the details and I am sitting here telling you that I really don't like most long-term insurance policies. If they don't have cost of living adjustments or are full of limitations, they are usually valueless by the time you need to use the benefits. However, properly formatted, they can prove useful.

Getting a program of this sort off the ground won't happen by itself. It also won't happen if only a private foundation attempts it as an experiment. That effort might have good intentions and certainly, if it works, it will be an example to point to, but the main thrust has to come from a larger entity, and the most logical is a state's arts agency, with federal support behind the scenes.

I envision a program spearheaded by the government which could suit the needs of artists and which could actually make a difference by creating 'arts districts' all across the United States.

My Trial Example

POSSIBLE PROGRESS AFTER YOU ARE GONE

I keep saying that you need to do things for yourself, while you are alive. No one will have the knowledge or incentive that you have.

You also need to think about your art as a business, in sober terms. Is there a market value? Will people want to come and see your art? Is your art practical and can it sell, or is your art very complex and not saleable? Is it good?

If you are making plans about what happens after you are gone, do you have sufficient funds to carry out your wishes? Are there ways to economize? Can your operating plan become more efficient? Do you have alternative plans?

There is a chance that, properly set up, your art could become more popular. However, it will take a lot of work to get to that point.

For example, among my thousands of works, many are on paper. For the past eight years, I've attended a weekly evening drawing group, where we share a model. Each session, I produce between 15 and 18 drawings. I go for about six months of the year, and so if I count an average of 15 drawings, times 26 weeks, times 8 years, I've created over 3,000 drawings.

Just an arbitrary few of the 3,000 figure drawings, in studio storage.

I have a routine; when I come home in the late evening, I spread my drawings out on the floor so if they are damp, they can dry completely. The next morning, I take a look at them, fresh, because I never have time to really look at them when I've just completed them - I'm immediately starting the next one. I then quickly pick up my favorite drawing, then my next favorite, and so forth. This is not a careful selection; my picks are approximate and quick, but there are some drawings that stand out and others I'm less excited about. I take the pile of drawings and put them away. The next week, I repeat the process and slowly the pile of drawings builds up. Every year, I put the drawings into a large flat box, and store them in my studio.

I used to sell drawings with paintings and sculptures at various gallery shows, but I purposely stopped showing in commercial galleries in the 1980s in favor of making larger works for museum shows. My work was growing in size and becoming non-saleable. Because of this decision, sales dwindled over the years.

However, figurative drawings are quite appealing to a large audience. The drawings to which I've been referring are larger than 20 x 30 inches, and when properly framed with extra wide matte, the framed works measure about 42 x 52 inches. For most homes, this is a large, impressive object to hang on a wall. I am realistic to know that I can't easily sell them without gallery promotion. So they remain in piles in my studio storage room.

Here's what I think can happen. As a bonus plan, I've envisioned using these drawings to help pay for my mini-museum. If the framing can be done in-house for $250, the drawings could be offered for sale for $750. In today's market, that's a reasonable price for a large, nicely framed original artwork, especially if marketed under the right conditions.

I hope that a curator, or arts management students will someday go through my piles. The first step would be to photograph and record the drawings. Each drawing should be labeled with a sticker (the drawings are dated with month and year) that shows the order in the pile (so each drawing from one evening drawing session would have a month, year, then have a number from 1 to 15, 16, or whatever the total number drawings from that session which shows my preference in selecting which ones I liked best, as well as some indication that it was a week of the month that was different from another week of the same month (so the month of October might have had several drawing sessions that month, and the labels could have 1. week, 2. week, 3. week, and so forth). The label should be placed on the front corner of the drawing as it is being photographed (or the drawings can be labeled digitally), and the label should be attached to the back of the drawing. This way, a permanent and accurate record is made.

Now for the purpose of the Rudd Art Museum, perhaps 200 or more drawings should be kept. I would recommend all number #1s be kept, and perhaps all the #2s, along with a few complete sessions to show an evening's output. The rest could be put up for sale.

For example, perhaps all the drawings marked #3 and #4 and #5 could be offered for sale first. That would represent 600 (1/5 of 3,000) drawings just to begin with. If the museum were opened, then my bet is that people would be more inclined to purchase an original large drawing from someone who has his own museum. If a modest 50 drawings could be framed and sold during one season/year, with a net of $500 (because the rest would pay for materials and labor for the framing), then that's $25,000 income that could be made. If 2,000 drawings were eventually sold over a period of years with a net profit of $500 each, then that would translate to $1 million dollars.

It could be an interesting semester's work for students, guided by an instructor, to carefully go through the drawings, do the archival work in preparing the records, then possibly go through the framing process to frame at least 50 of them as a pilot program. Because all that woodworking equipment and space are available in the conservation area of my studio-turned-museum , this actually would be a wonderful teaching project for an arts management class.

That's how I see it. However, I could be wrong - the drawings might not sell. Then the basic museum plan would have to work on its own. If the drawings could be sold, the proceeds would just become added income for the overall operation, perhaps supplying sufficient income to pay for the main staff person.

The point is, that the formation of the museum could give the art a much greater chance of bringing in sales, than would occur if a dealer, or lawyer, or agent were to try to unload them upon my death. In all frankness, I doubt that anyone would buy them under rushed circumstances. So figuring out a way to promote the artist could pay off in other ways. But in the meantime, I need to figure out a way to finance the overall program that in turn would prepare the drawings and ready them to archive, to exhibit and to sell. To make this income a possibility, I need to first figure out a way to have a facility open for many years, in order to sell the works gradually. If my number is 2,000 works (and that represents only these figure drawings!), at 50 works per year, that's 40 years that a museum store would need to stay in business in order to sell the works. That just won't happen without having everything in place. But if I do the work to set up the foundation, then this supply of reasonably priced original works of art could be a welcome income stream.

MY HISTORY

I will only give you a brief history of my own experience here; for a fuller description of how I went about it, I invite you to read my books, The Art World Dream and The Art Studio/Loft Manual (now available as e-books).

In a nutshell, being forced out of a very large and very cheap studio in Washington D.C. because the landlord wanted to convert the building, I managed to buy a 34,000 square foot warehouse in the 'other side of town.' Even for the time (1978), it was reasonable, only $66,000, and it came with seller financing. I was in a state of shock when I discovered that I was unable to afford the heat, after seeing the tanks empty having just filled them with oil a few days earlier, I began to sub-let spaces in order to share the cost of operating the large building. Soon thereafter and with a bank loan, I did a complete renovation of the building, dividing it into twenty artists studios and lofts-- the first such industrial loft and studio building ever done in Washington DC.

I kept 14,000 square feet for myself, surely the largest studio in the city (greatly surpassing my previous 6,000 square foot studio), but after a few years, the studio filled to the point where either things had to go into the dumpster to create new art, or I couldn't work. (Securing additional storage space created it's own strains.)

That began my dream of having sufficient space - and permanent space - whereby studio moves and dumpster thoughts would not be on my mind. At the same time, I had wild plans for future art installations that would require not only space, but substantial financial investment-- something that I didn't want to do if the effort was only for a temporary exhibition. I started to look for abundant but cheap studio space-- almost anywhere in the country.

Serendipitously, when a sculpture residency in 1987 at G.E. Plastics introduced me to the Berkshires and mill spaces, I was able to purchase at a bargain basement price (if I told you how cheap, you wouldn't believe me, so I won't bother!) a huge industrial mill in the blue collar, distressed town of North Adams, the projected home of a proposed new art museum. That museum had a roller coaster ride for ten more years before it opened to the public in 1999 as MASS MoCA, the Massachusetts Museum of Contemporary Art.

The 130,000 square foot, historic Beaver Mill, home of Rudd Studio and loft, as well as other artist studios. North Adams, MA. (photo by Kelly Lee)

So in 1990, I sub-divided and leased my 14,000 square foot Washington D.C. studio and moved into half of the 130,000 square foot Beaver Mill (that's like three full football fields under roof), while I rented out the other half of the mill to various artists and commercial tenants.   In order for you to realize that this is not beyond the means of an average person, I did all these things on a shoestring budget. The move to the Beaver Mill was scary, but even with just a few tenants, I started with and maintained a positive cash flow.

That's it in a nutshell-- but along the way, my idea of having permanent exhibition space for my large-scale art projects stayed with me and evolved.

Now that I've reached my 'senior" status, that evolution has continued and has stimulated new uses of the space.

A FEW YEARS LATER

The SFMoMA, has 7,000 paintings and sculptures in their collection; other large museums have similar quantities in their collections. Each museum has a full staff to store, preserve, exhibit and deal with its collection, in addition to other art brought in for new shows.

I've never counted, but including works on paper, I'll bet that I have almost that many works, now housed in part of my studio of about 50,000 square feet (with the ability to expand as finances permit). But I have a staff of no one-- well, I have a part-time maintenance person with helper if I need to move something heavy or just need some assistance for an hour - but that doesn't start to compare with the staff that even a medium or small art museum might have.

So while I probably have one of the largest spaces in the United States, I don't have the resources that one might expect. As I'm sure many artists dream, I often day dream, "if only I were famous......" If my work sold for several hundred thousands of dollars each, there's no doubt I could hire the necessary staff to preserve my art as well as help me create new work.

However, I'm lucky that I do have some resources and that I have so much space. The question that has gnawed at me increasingly over the years is, who will oversee this unwieldy "empire" when I'm gone? How do I protect my work, and can it ever be shown to the public. Only a star artist like "Warhol" or "Rauschenberg" would have the financial ability to fund a private museum. For stars, museums would also invite the art to go there for a permanent exhibition format.

Private museums of this sort usually have an endowment to go with the art-- and both enable the museum to operate. I don't have that type of financial strength. However, I do have one very important component - I purchased an excess of space at cheap, cheap prices. With rental income, I was able to renovate and upgrade the infrastructure over the years.

In the case of the historic Beaver Mill, my concept is simple. In very rough terms, I think that half of the building, including most of the floors that now serve as my studio and storage, could be converted into public museum space. The other half of the building could be rented so that the rental income would support the public aspect. In a sense, the extra space becomes my endowment.

While in theory this could work out, it would have to be done very economically within the constraints of that limited income. But there are several nearby examples. In the Berkshires, the major art museums are the Norman Rockwell Museum (in southern Berkshire county), and near me, the Clark Art Institute, Williams College Museum of Art and the Massachusetts Museum of Contemporary Art (MASS MoCA). Those museums are open year-round with impressive attendance, but they receive more than three quarters of their visitors during the six warmest months of the year.

Interestingly, in addition to the Normal Rockwell Museum that is of course dedicated to one artist, MASS MoCA has a separate 27,000 square foot building devoted solely to the work of Sol LeWitt. The exhibition is scheduled to last twenty-five years. Although a part of the museum, it feels like a single-artist museum as it occupies a separate wing of the museum.

However, there are at least two other serious museums in the region that are only open during the high season. A house-turned-museum, Frelinghuysen Morris House and Studio, is open just during the summer and fall months, and closes for the winter season. The second is Chesterwood, the home and studio of Daniel Chester French, the sculptor of the Lincoln Memorial. Both are successful attractions and they simply concentrate their visitors into the high (warm) season. A seasonal format would be possible for the proposed Rudd Art Museum as well. There is no way that a museum on a modest budget can justify heating acres of space for very few winter visitors.

In 2000, I purchased a beautiful church for the price of an upscale car, mostly to prevent it from crumbling during the next winter. With modest repairs, I was able to preserve the building. North Adams continued to have a distressed economy, and so with no prospective renters or buyers for the church, I decided to move into the church a large figurative installation that had been occupying a lot of space in my studio. It consisted of 150 life-sized figures. I then decided to expand the installation by doing the ceiling (my own Sistine Chapel?).

In any case, I relate all this because at that point, I had a completed installation that could be open to the public. I inaugurated the exhibition one cold winter day in December 2001 with a fireplace opening (the only heat source), and since then, I've had it open to the public each summer. It was named "A Chapel for Humanity" as suggested by my friend, the late Walter Hopps who was director of the Menil Collection, which incidentally has the only major-artist chapel in the U.S in a style very much different from mine. The "Rothko Chapel" is very Zen-like while my chapel is very baroque.

A Chapel for Humanity opened in 2001, and is open free to the public during the summer and fall. It has been operated for more than a decade as a single-artist museum/alternative space on a shoestring budget and with minimum labor.

Maintaining my chapel exhibition has come with its usual small annoyances, like 'staffing' it, opening and closing it each day, and normal repairs and upkeep. We live in such a small town, and as of yet, it remains somewhat dysfunctional in getting MoCA museum visitors to go a block or two into the downtown area (including to my Chapel). With insufficient visitors, I can't afford or justify having either a paid staff person or even a volunteer docent, because the job would be too boring. So I purchased a Radio Shack camera and placed a sign on the desk at the entrance and pretend that there is a staff person who is "away for a moment."

I do not charge admission because it would not pay to staff someone for that purpose - although I do see that changing in the years ahead, as the town is beginning to understand how to be a tourist-town. Once in a while, when the chapel is closed, I get a call from a visitor on a cell phone asking to be let in; I simply tell the visitors where the key is hidden and allow them to let themselves in, and I ask them to please lock afterwards.

With sadness, I've watched the security videos as thieves would cut open the plastic jar and take as little as $1; never more than $10 is kept in the donation jar. That's just a statement about the economic times in which we live, but never has anyone broken one of the sculptures in the more than ten years that the exhibition has been open.

In a sense, I've been running a small museum on an extremely modest scale for the past decade. As I've experimented, the town slowly - painfully slowly to me - has been evolving and catching on to the fact that we need to tap into MASS MoCA's visitors in a better way. With a new mayor came a breath of fresh air; the town is steadily improving and I can be patient a little while longer. I think in a year, there'll be a big difference, but no matter whether it takes two years or five years or even ten years, I know that conditions will steadily improve and that the town will increase it's lure as a cultural tourist destination.

From my perspective in trying to imagine what will happen in another twenty years, I'm confident that North Adams will be a hub of artistic activity. I've been preaching for twenty years that North Adams will become a cultural theme park-- with MASS MoCA serving as the big draw- the big "roller-coaster" and other sites, including A Chapel for Humanity and other art spaces, constituting the other "ride" attractions.

So I have as possible future museum sites this church and my mill. I recently made one more expansive move. I purchased another bargain, a much larger stone church at the top of Main Street, and a stone's throw from A Chapel for Humanity (see the next section). With these three properties, I can put together a vast exhibition of my work.

And I have one important advantage-- whatever my plans are for preserving and exhibiting my art after my death, there is no urgent timetable. My joke is, that upon death, I'll have a lot of patience. If I have goals that I think can be implemented gradually, whether that takes two years or twenty years is of little consequence to me. I'll be resting comfortably underground, so to speak.

MY CURRENT SITUATION

Sometimes one needs to jump on a real estate opportunity. Other times, you can walk away and come back years later and get an even better deal. That has been the case in North Adams, despite MASS MoCA's success.

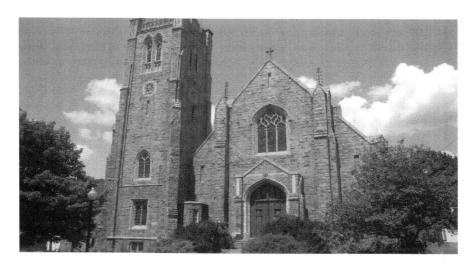

A new purchase: this 20,000 square foot stone church on Main Street, North Adams, only three blocks from MASS MoCA. Purchased for $5 per sq. foot, this can be a perfect artist museum space!

Very recently, I purchased (not a secret- it was for sale for more than two years) a 20,000 square foot, beautiful stone church that is in the middle of our downtown. It is in incredible condition, needing only a little work (of course, one could spend much more depending on one's appetite). How much? $125,000 and it came with financing!

Now even if you think that's expensive, understand what this would cost if five artists went in on it together-- just $25,000 each. Each artist could have used in one fashion or another, 4,000 square feet for $25,000, and this is just a couple of blocks away from MASS MoCA, right in the middle of town! Think about what type of house you can buy for $125,000. In this church I have something, that in today's money, would cost perhaps $10 to $20 million to replicate. If that's not enough reason to convince you, then nothing will. Think how many artists there are between Boston and New York City! All of them could have made use of this building, 2.5 to 3 hours away in the middle of the Berkshires!

If I didn't already have great residential loft and studio, I could have easily moved into this church and met all my needs, with a total expenditure that would exceed by very little that for an attractive house in the area.

Since I'm not living there, I need to look at it in different terms - as an extra project. I don't have the financial strength to carry all this on my own; but my concept is simple- I want to use the main sanctuary space, with its 30-foot ceiling, for an installation of my blow-molded polycarbonate sculptures, set upon a crisp giant iceberg-like mound split into three parts so viewers can walk between the sections to get closer to the sculptures. As I concentrate on the big sanctuary installation, I am reserving the remainder of the spaces for other non-profit users, including possibly (as I write this) the local history museum for its new home, for the Chamber of Commerce and for a visitors' center. Hopefully, these types of tenants will keep it as a public space that will be staffed and that will carry the load of maintenance, debt and utilities, while I add to my museum offerings.

I could operate the entire building on a shoestring as only the Rudd Art Museum; that's my backup option. It could be open just half the year, so no heat would be needed. It's owned by a foundation, so no real estate taxes are paid. I have minimal maintenance and just as I've operated my "A Chapel for Humanity" exhibition for the past decade, these two spaces could be the gateway museums until the "Mother Lode" is ready at the Beaver Mill. Ultimately, it is possible that I might have the Rudd Art Museum #1, #2, and #3.

The total combined space to be used for museum exhibition purposes is very large indeed. The foundation can use whatever portion of the total space as it can afford. The less space it uses, the more space can be rented out to insure income. Even on the lower end, it does bring the net exhibition space into the big leagues. For example, the Warhol Museum in Pittsburgh has 88,000 square feet. Size doesn't make it important but size allows for an incredible array of displays and installations on a permanent or semi-permanent basis. Size allows for critical mass, which in itself will make the museum more worthwhile for someone to visit -there'll just be more to see for the same ticket price. Size also will stimulate additional publicity, which will make it better known. On the downside, largest means more maintenance concerns, to some degree.

MY FUTURE VISION

Ok, here's my dream. I'm 90 years old or so, still alive and kicking and still creating in my studio. There's the Rudd Art Museum 1, 2 and 3. Two are churches, one containing abstract plastic polycarbonate and robotic sculptures, the other housing my figurative installation. The headquarters at the historic Beaver Mill becomes a museum of 70,000 square feet of exhibition space (also containing my storage and preservation areas) but while I'm alive or in residence, only half to two-thirds of the space is open to the public for at least half of the year. That allows me to continue to work. Some of the private studio space that I'm still using can also be in operation as the museum-study center. The Arts Management program of the nearby Massachusetts College of Liberal Arts (I stimulated that program more than a dozen years ago and now it's their pride and joy) has students who can serve as interns to staff the museum during fall weekends and daily during summer months. Each winter and spring semester, there's a small group of future curators, guided by an instructor, that accesses the storage areas and assembles art from one period of my work, digitizes and catalogs the group's research, puts it in historical context, installs an exhibition for the summer that focuses on this aspect of my work, and then selects a few pieces that might be merged into the permanent retrospective of my art. And they can get additional first-hand information from me because I'll be there! In addition, this group might help curate an independent exhibition of work by other artists who can be academically related to my work. After all, my work by the time I'm 90 years of age represents three quarters of a century, and there are many ways to put that span of work into historical context.

That's my vision and my dream.

THE SHORTCOMINGS

What are the shortcomings? Money, money and money. That's the main thing. Even with money, it is hard to write an ironclad legal will so that my vision will be carried out exactly as I specify. And who knows--perhaps others will be able to improve upon my vision - so maybe it's best not to be too rigid with my demands. But more often than not, things deteriorate. Without sufficient funds, this can happen easily.

Without careful monitoring, people can overspend quickly and dry up the limited resources. I fear the day when my art is consolidated into one storage space somewhere, buildings are sold and I'm soon forgotten. I'll be dead so I won't care, but that's not my intention for my art while I'm still in control.

Of course, the other main shortcoming is securing that key person who can carry out my vision without depleting my limited assets. Finding the right manager is tricky, and I won't be around to make changes. So in a sense, I'll have to have a foundation board that is willing to keep a watchful eye on things. The hope, of course, is that the foundation and operation settles into a workable routine, before the original team transitions. I'm hoping for a 'long run,' and that means several generations of managers and trustees.

The main solution is to have a solid structure, with goals that are well within the financial capacity of the foundation. As wild as I am, I can become very conservative when I put on my financial glasses.

SOMETIMES THERE'S NO CHOICE

Judd, Chamberlain, Rauschenberg, Warhol had completed a lot of large artworks over the decades. Their market value is so great that there is more than sufficient demand for their work. Whether it's simply placement in museums, or controlled by foundations with a specific place to display a lot of their work (as in the case of Judd and Warhol, for examples), their estates have it made by comparison to the rest of the art world.

There remain, however, tens of thousands, if not hundreds of thousands, of respectable artists who also have an abundance of work still in their possession, but do not have the market strength to have their work easily sold or placed when they are gone.

Especially for post-World War II American artists who have worked large and proficiently, studios are filled to the brim. I know that I am probably at the top edge of this group in terms of how much art I have and the size of my work. Over the years,

I've gradually expanded my studio space to both accommodate my need to make additional large pieces, but also to simply store the ones already completed. Some of these pieces have been exhibited at least once but didn't sell and thus continue to "reside" with me.

Included among the thousands of artworks, I have dozens, and probably hundreds of sculptural works that range in size from large refrigerators to a herd of elephants to several that might be in the dinosaur-size class. I have several works that, as installations, take up museum-sized spaces. The easier ones are the two-dimensional paintings and wall reliefs, but many of these measure 16 to 20 feet in width, and are about half that high in height.

To take just one of these and to try to place it is practically impossible. No home will have sufficient interior space. My materials, in most cases, do not allow these sculptures to be placed in outdoor spaces, which might be easier to acquire than for interior spaces. Commercial spaces such as lobbies of office buildings are less spacious than in the past and now demand premium rents. From the point of view of permanency, security (my art is not child-proof nor made for unsupervised public display) and aesthetics, my work is not that appealing to the average corporate executive. Of course, I'd love to have more pieces in museum collections, but few museums will take art of this size, even if my reputation might warrant it.

In plain words, I'm dead-in-the-water. Many of my larger pieces are my "jewels." After all, I've been working close to that half-century mark-- that's a lot of years of working hard, and the results literally pile up.

I'm not alone. I know there exists a sizable number of artists in the country who are in this same predicament. That is why so many studios are filled to the brink, in the same way that closets get crammed with so much stuff that will astonish you once you pull everything out and see how it fills the room. Over the years, artists stuff nooks and crannies with their art. Some rent extra storage spaces, many have built special storage racks, others have art in various places all over town, often with friends with "special arrangements," and almost all have completed work crammed into their working studio.

As long as the artist is alive and healthy, he or she can continue to juggle the balls in the air. But at some point, everything will come crashing down. Unfortunately, this can happen at the worse possible time (for example, if you are forced out of your studio or storage facility) or it will happen upon death, when the same problems get dumped onto someone else.

After many years of accumulation, I own sufficient space that I could arrange to simply take a floor and squeeze every single piece of my art into that space, arrange to give someone the key and give instructions about how to "place" my works - and hope for the best. The sure answer will be that the art will collect dust, and in a few decades, no one will care. At some point in the future, when money runs out, a contractor with crew will come in and "clean out the space." All that "stuff" will simply go into dumpsters to be hauled away. That will be the end of a half-century of art creation.

This is a horrible vision, of course. But the only recourse is to make the arrangements now so that my work can be stored and handled, and at least some of it can be exhibited, hopefully on a rotating schedule to allow more of the work to be seen over time. In addition, if there's work available to place elsewhere or to sell to suitable parties (depending on price and/or prestige), then someone needs to be around who can effectively handle that role. Of course, everyone would hope that all this could be done within a reasonable time period, such as over ten years, but if I haven't been able to place/sell more than a fraction of my work over a half century, why would I have the expectation that someone else can do a better job when I'm gone?

It is with this sober view that I basically conclude, perhaps in my defense, that there is no other choice. I have to determine my own destiny with what I've created during my lifetime.

Old Power

POWER TO THE OLD FOLKS

The older we are, the more our connections dry up (our friends in high places retire or die). At the same time, often we do have connections with people who have risen up in the ranks. Therefore, we have a greater ability to make a call or send an email to someone who has influence. The same can be said about political connections and business contacts at larger corporations.

The question is how to best use these connections? Do you want to influence politics to get funding for artists in general? Or do you want to get support for a large project in which you might have a role? Do you want corporate sponsorship to carry out your ideas?

I've often gone to corporations that have the materials or processes that were well beyond my financial reach. The best example occurred in 1987 when I asked G.E. Plastics for help. They generously responded by giving me access to a million dollar plastic blow-molder, giving me 4,000 pounds of Lexan, and giving me a week of work time with an operator and engineer. I was back several times after that first residency, and I continue to access the new corporate entity that purchased that division.

As we age, and as our projects often become larger and/or more critical, and perhaps as they become our permanent memorials and highlights of our working careers, sponsorship can make the critical difference. Museums actively seek corporate sponsors. Once they have them, the sponsors are prominently portrayed on the walls and in the catalogs. There is no reason not to take this same approach.

Being a big fish in a small pond has benefits that artists won't find in larger communities. Often the real estate is cheaper, it's easier and faster to get services (although the number of options may be reduced), and you can connect with executives, authorities and town councils about your art project. Regional corporate entities may look favorably towards your idea once you pitch them in a positive way. At the same time, smaller or more rural regions may not be as knowledgeable or experienced with the arts. A cultural proposal might sound quite foreign to them.

When we moved to the small town of North Adams, I remember being invited into scores of local organizations, from the Chamber of Commerce to the Art Technology Task Force. All groups in town were trying to ascertain the impact that the proposed new art museum might have to the city. As the only "new" artist in town, I was invited to join and help with their research and deliberations. Of course I knew the impact and benefits that a major new art museum would likely have, but I was patient to work with civic leaders who had little knowledge or initial interest about art.

During one meeting, I'll never forget when one businessman, long involved in town development, turned to me and said, "Eric, you must think we are still in the dark ages, but compared to where we have come from, we have advanced light years." So, you too, might have to take on the role of educator as you introduce new ideas about art, and if necessary, work patiently with town officials and concerned citizens. In the end, they will hopefully be your strongest supporters.

As "senior artists," we might not get respect from younger artists, but we do seem to get more respect from lay people than a young "upstart" might. That means we can talk to corporations, retail and wholesale businesses, manufacturers, city councils, town clubs, schools, universities and politicians. I've given art talks to everyone from the Rotary to the Garden Club - all are active in my region. We seniors are mature and knowledgeable, so we have a better ability to talk to the people from whom we want support in order to get our foot in the door. Older artists can be a powerful voice if we know where to focus our energy.

SOME HAVE MONEY

I'm assuming that all artists are struggling to some extent. We make art that mostly won't sell. Our expenses might be tax write-offs, but I constantly complain that one needs income to offset and make use of the deductions.

However, many older Americans do have some money; some get inheritances, others have saved as a result both spouses having worked, and many others have benefited from the greatest real estate appreciation in history and hopefully didn't get wiped out a few years ago.

If this is the case, then older folks do have the security to invest or spend their money for substantial projects. For every artist whom I used to see going to the gas or electric company to pay a bill before the disconnection date, I've seen an equal number of others who have no issue with spending funds for world travel, nice cars and a generous life style.

Old age is the time to decide what's important. Using available resources certainly can put into action many of the ideas presented in this book.

Some Conclusions

WHO WILL CARE?

Let me state the obvious. No one, and I mean *no one*, will care about your art as much as you do. Well, if you are unlucky enough to die young enough so that your spouse is young enough to handle your estate, then perhaps he or she will be devoted enough and smart enough to push your art as you would have wanted it to be promoted. But if you are lucky, and your spouse is equally lucky, you will both be in your old age by the time you go; should you go first, then your spouse at an advanced age will not be able to deal with it. And, in likelihood, neither will your kids.

If you have a reputation and your art really has some value, then someone might come along who has a real interest. The natural person would be a gallery dealer who knows how to market your art. But believe me when I say that the gallery agent will have, as a primary interest, the desire to liquidate your art so as to produce income. That's the gallery's business, after all. A byproduct of that could be to enhance your reputation if, by advancing your art, the gallery were to realize additional sales at higher prices. But again, your art needs to have been critically recognized as having achieved a fairly high level and to have had a proven track record in order for these things to fall into line.

The people who normally end up with the liability of handling your art will most likely not be art professionals who care one bit about it except to get rid of it expediently. They will be the lawyers and financial advisors. Alternatively, it will land in the lap of a family member not equipped to deal with it. That's not what you'd like to happen, I'm sure.

No one will work for free, outside of a close family member. The less money involved, the less of a quality job someone will do. That's human nature. So your art needs to be worth enough and be generating cash to pay for whomever will assist in the final distribution.

The only way to prevent a miserable aftermath is to take preventive action yourself. This will entail a lot of work and a lot of planning. The earlier you start, the better.

Even if you are very modest with regard to the worth of your art, in dollar terms or in terms of "leaving it for humanity," you probably still want a sensible distribution of your art after you die. And to rely on your spouse is both unrealistic and unfair.

Many artists have mentioned that such and such an organization would take their art, but that's usually just wishful thinking.

Even with a desire to have an organization handle the art, what is the rationale for some organization accepting your work? Does your art have a relationship to what that organization is doing, or its history? Did you have a personal relationship with that organization?

No organization will want your art unless you provide enough cash to support the expenses of dealing with it-- in terms of taking physical delivery and including all the administration that is involved in making an inventory and then trying to distribute, store, preserve, sell or dispose of it.

ARTISTS ARE NOT ALWAYS SMART

I don't want to insult anyone, but when thinking about and getting excited about some possible projects that will help many artists, and setting examples for the rest of the country, I know that it's not easy to convince artists who have never had these ideas introduced to them. This is one of the biggest failures of art schools and university art departments. Long-term planning, real estate knowledge, and studio management should be as much a part of learning as basic painting, drawing and art concepts.

I say this because an idea that needs the participation of twenty artists, and that would really give those twenty artists incredible opportunities, should be an "easy sell," but it's not. I think it is difficult - but not impossible - to get twenty artists to jointly participate. Certainly, it would be so much easier, for example, if the Guggenheim initiated this concept on as a pilot program to help serious artists. Man, then artists would be banging down the door to get aboard! A big name curator/museum/artist would give it instant credibility. Maybe that could be arranged. If not, it would simply take the courage and ambition of a small group of artists. If twenty artists with a strong conviction and vision would take this on, then by setting a positive example, there could be a chain reaction across the United States. I'm an optimist, but it has to start from somewhere. I'm hoping that this book becomes the spark.

It will take some initial organization; since securing a physical space is essential, financing might be tricky but then again, perhaps there'll be seller financing for the purchase of the real estate. It will take leadership. It will take an extra effort to plan it out, but none of it is that difficult. The basic outline of a proposal could be done in a few days and then artists could be selected. Quality of art is essential, in my view, to set the bar high.

I can't tell you how much I tried to make this happen two decades ago. I wanted to do a similar idea with the Eclipse Mill twenty years ago, but I couldn't convince even five artists to go in together to purchase another mill building. I eventually went into it alone and I have enjoyed the fruits (and also headaches) of having taken that risk. But I felt then, as I do now, that the risk was minimal because what I've been proposing is to purchase space in quantity, at a cheap price and near major cultural attractions, so that something creative and special can occur. That's how history is often made, by just a few people doing something daring. In the case of the Eclipse Mill, about a decade later, the mill was still for sale, but for less than before, so I purchased it and did I ever have a stampede! However, I had to be the one to organize it, and to offer manageable units (2,000 to 3,000 square feet) for reasonable prices. I could never have convinced those same 60 artists (or even 10 of them) to join me as co-developers. But I wonder-- now that I've set one example, and there are other examples in the United States, might artists wise up and see new types of opportunities? I'll know that artists have gotten smarter if and when I learn that a small group has taken over an abandoned Wal-Mart or other big box store somewhere in the United States.

And I suggest this with tongue in cheek, because I want artists to get angry that they aren't taking charge of their lives. Someone could say that what I'm suggesting is perfect for only a young artist, just finding his or her voice, and not for older artists. To the contrary - I'm suggesting that it's even more suited for the mature artist, who has some financial ability to find the investment money that will allow him or her to attempt this sort of a daring expansion.

KNOWING YOUR WORK WILL BE IN A MUSEUM MIGHT MAKE YOU WORK BETTER

If you know that every painting that you create will sell for $250,000, will you take a bit more time? Go to a bit more trouble? Use some better materials?

Human nature is such that we tend to get a bit casual about how we work. But if the work is heading for a major collection, or even a museum show, might you put a bit more effort into the work? Now I can argue that I put maximum effort into all my art, whether it's a drawing or a major sculpture, but I know that my attitude changes slightly if the work is heading for some prominent place. As I get older and I start to narrow down the scope of my work, I start thinking more about the pieces that will get the most effect. I'm less interested in creating another dozen works just to put them into storage; I'd rather work on one or two larger works that might end up being the masterpieces (not to equate big with better).

The idea that you might create your own museum space for the purpose of showing the best of your art might just stimulate you to concentrate on those ambitious projects that you really want to realize, but maybe you just haven't gotten around to them. This is not a sure bet, but thinking about this idea might prove to be a positive stimulation for your art.

EGO/VANITY OR SENSIBLE?

I am evaluating my own art and giving it a value-- a historical value. If I were a Warhol or Rauschenberg, there would be enough museum directors underscoring my Rudd Art Museum plans. But I'm not of that fame. So can this be viewed as just a big ego project? Will anyone really care when it's all said and done? I am advocating for other artists to follow these same steps, whether it's on a grand scale or on a small scale. But is it just artificially holding up something that the "art world" has already not recognized as being among the best contemporary art of our time? After all, if it were that good, wouldn't it already be recognized as such?

I have a very respectable bio; my work is in the collection of a dozen notable museums. I'm in quite a few collections and I've sold my art for fairly hefty prices. So is there a specific number of collections/museums/prices that I have to reach in order for this museum concept to be considered acceptable?

These issues do bother me, because I don't want those kinds of accusations. I will get them, no doubt, especially from jealous artists who think I'm jumping ahead of them in an unfair way. They will think to themselves that we are all competing for curatorial and museum attention, and we should all play the system according to the current rules. They will feel that I am going outside of the playbook, and somehow using unfair advantages. I know this because I have heard the objections in many forms about some of my past projects. They will say that I, and others who follow in my footsteps, are just 'buying' our way to the top. In some ways, that's true, but I started with nothing and did it by focusing on my art ambitions. And in fairness, I have the same feelings when I see big-name artists getting those $300,000 public sculpture commissions; I'm sure that on a similar budget I could also do a sensational piece, but I won't have that chance. I also feel that way when I see retrospective exhibitions in major museums by artists whom I don't feel deserve the show any more than I do. But yes, for many artists, I'm viewed as being in the same big leagues. However, the only reason I can even think about having permanent museum space is that I had that vision, saved and manipulated toward that goal, and bought bargain real estate spaces that could do "double-duty," serving as residence, work space, storage space, experimental exhibition space, and finally, as a permanent "memorial" for my life's work.

Some artists have expressed feelings that artists who can afford to establish a foundation should spend their money to help others, and not themselves. I think for the larger foundations with deep pockets that might be warranted. But I have nothing against funds being used to study, preserve, and promote the original artist's art as being the primary mission of that artist's foundation. To me, it's just an alternative art space with an archival-study center overlay.

In the end, I don't really care about public opinion; I must live the way I feel I should. That's been the rule I've followed which has led on the path to making the kind of art I make - I have always gone my own route, alone, in a way contrary to popular trends. This has hurt me commercially in the past, but I have enjoyed creating art that is unique, and in ways such that no other artist has come close to my style-- using new materials and technologies and processes.

DON'T TRY TO TEST THE DEMAND/MARKET

A few decades ago, I was having serious financial problems. I wanted to throw in the towel and move to another place in the country to start afresh. I had a family to worry about but I thought we could make the change. My more immediate problem was a large studio full of art. It felt like an anchor around my leg. Then I had an inspiration - if you want to call it that; another description might be 'reckless abandonment.' In any case, I thought of renting out the Corcoran Museum, which one could do for special events. I was going to have a one-weekend-only going-out-of-business sale. All paintings, no matter what size, would be $100 to $200 (can't remember anymore) and all drawings were going to be $25. The idea was to advertise this big "art happening" and I thought I could get a crowd of people hauling off $10,000 paintings for $200. I was going to liquidate and take the proceeds to jumpstart my new life.

The problem was, it was just an illusion. There was no chance that more than a few dozen people would come. After all, who could use a 16-foot wide painting for their house? I realized, after careful (and more rational) consideration, that while a dealer could sell a painting of mine for thousands of dollars once in a blue moon, in a rushed situation, I couldn't give it away even for free, if my life depended on it.

Eventually, I climbed out of my economic canyon, bit by bit. But the idea about how much my art really was worth in the art market was a revelation, and not necessarily a happy one. When someone puts down a value for something on a bank statement, for example, it's usually referred to as fair market value (FMV). That implies what a willing buyer would pay to a willing seller in a reasonable time period. But if you have to liquidate, and you have lots of art, and the demand is weak, prices will fall, and often, you can't even give it away. In fact, often owners have to pay someone to haul away things that should have value, but there isn't, especially at the time you need it. Particularly in the United States, we are a disposable society. Our culture is to throw away and simply buy a replacement, which is often improved.

That's the same problem that exists at the time of an artist's death. The estate, consisting of unsold art, papers, equipment and things collected, often doesn't have real market value. That's not to say the art isn't good and shouldn't have value. It's just a realistic assessment of the real world and about what the public will buy at the moment.

Walter Hopps liked to talk to me about Vincent Van Gogh, as an example of market timing. It's well known that the artist only sold one canvas in his lifetime. Depressed, he finally killed himself. Of course, his works are now treasured as masterpieces. What most people don't know is, if Vincent had just stayed alive another six months, his work would have started selling like crazy. All around, collectors had finally caught up with the innovative artists of the day. If he had just stayed around, he would have been part of this upswing in the art market. He would have been a respected and reasonably affluent artist within a year. His sales had nothing to do with his death but only about what was happening in the marketplace. The moral of the story is that market timing can change. It might not happen in your lifetime, it might happen some years later. Certainly, there are many examples of artists' estates, which have appreciated substantially since the artist's death.

I like the idea of "single-artist" museums. Some might call them vanity museums, as they label some collections that have gone public. In fifty years, they won't be called that. But no matter which opinion someone has about whether it's for vanity or not, if the space contains good art, having it for public display will be worthwhile.

So I grow a thick skin, and persevere. And I urge others to follow, as this could become a new trend in the art world. It only takes a dozen or so ambitious projects for the idea to become a trend, and a trend will be reported and once reported nationally, there will be a stampede. I don't doubt that.

THE LAST PERSON STANDING WINS

Often work that survives has more value. Work that has disappeared is forgotten about, for obvious reasons. The point I'm making is that there are lots of artists today who are mentioned frequently in the art magazines, but in a century's time, they will be largely forgotten. Their work might be relegated to the museums' basements over time, seeing the light of the gallery bulbs less and less. Paintings that were sold to people will survive and some will get into collections if the value holds up, but if not, then they'll also disappear over time. They will be in various homes, or eventually be stored in attics and basements, perhaps eventually thrown away. In a hundred years, there might be value only for those that have historical significance, and since there has been so much art produced in the past century, not much of what has been produced can be filtered for value. That's just the way it is. A group of works, preserved for a hundred years on display, will have artistic value simply by being there - it's not always about who gets the most press now, it's about who will still be shown in a hundred years.

This is not to say that quality and relevance aren't major factors, but it's to acknowledge the many external factors that will influence the way that certain artworks get the attention and get remembered.

The high priests of the museum world do anoint specific works and artists and maintain the high status of these works and artists almost forever. To become a part of that limelight means that you need to duplicate some of the things museums do, such as showing the work in a respected space, stimulating documentation and critical writing about the work, and in a sense, doing promotional work although not in obvious ways. For example, a study by a curator is important; no one knows behind-the-scenes why a certain curator decided to study a certain artist - only that it happens. This is not a political campaign, although there are similarities. Dealers know how to play the game, as do sophisticated museums.

I've known a few artists who over the years collected and traded art. They ended up with valuable collections and eventually made a donation to a major museum of their collections, which included their own art. That is certainly an easier way through the front door. Museums are no different than politicians in this way, and they can be influenced by money.

Just as there are the major museums, there are hundreds of secondary (i.e. in size and quantity of art, not necessarily in quality) museums across the country, many private, many public or associated with colleges and universities. There are hundreds if not thousands of alternative spaces-- exhibition spaces that are not traditional retail galleries. These alternative spaces often evolve into more established museum formats, in some cases not for the better as increases in costs tend to steer them into more traditional roles in order to keep their funding coming in. Nevertheless, many play an exciting role and many have become stable and permanent.

I am suggesting that you, the individual artist or the collaborative group of artists, can establish such an 'alternative' art space. The real estate is out there for the picking; only the effort is needed to make this option a reality.

The key word in your efforts, however, should be "permanence." It is one thing to plan something that operates for a short time, or something that operates as long as you are the operator (which means being chief cook and bottle washer too). It is another thing to construct an operation that has a 50-year or longer timeline.

Again, work can be in expansive or in very restricted space, such as the 1979 installation of De Maria's "The Broken Kilometer," on West Broadway in New York City. This is an example of a non-museum permanent display of a single artist's work, supported by the family behind the Dia Art Foundation. New York is not cheap and therefore a space like this is not relevant for most artists, but there are other locations. This type of installation can be done in small towns all over the country, without needing a vast treasure chest.

How much would you know about De Maria's "The Broken Kilometer" if it had been shown once and was now in a museum's basement, to be installed every decade or two? Having it on permanent exhibition certainly helps! That is why I say that if your work can be preserved as a consequence of being on public display, it will by default be ahead of most other art that will naturally, over time, disappear from sight and mind.

GENERAL LAST ADVICE - BEFORE YOU DIE

While I hope that younger artists will read this book and become smart very early in their careers, I'm not that optimistic. The Art World Dream was written for the developing artist who is serious about managing his or her life while doing ambitious art.

I am assuming that you are on the "other" half of your life and career, although still young enough and energetic enough to carry out many ambitious projects and not afraid to reexamine your situation, your possibilities, and most of all, your desires.

As you might know after reading about what I've done, I'm an eternal optimist. I get excited about making art, and this excitement carries me through the often laborious, painstaking processes. I am ambitious about my art, and I never want to be restricted, certainly not by space or industrial processes. No one says that making art is fun. I've joked that it sure is a lot easier than hanging sheet rock for a living, but that doesn't make it easy. I think it was Neil Simon but probably many writers who said that if you want to know what is real work, just try facing a blank sheet of paper every day. I feel the same way. It is extremely difficult to face a blank canvas or a blank sketchpad and give birth to something that the world might view with wonder and admiration.

Once completed, art then is subject to many external variables, such as who sees it and when, one person's subjective decision about it, practical issues such as if it can be sold easily, and so forth. A career is made up of hundreds of these things, and how they get juggled can determine if you become famous or if you don't. But those variables are secondary aspects of the original creation. And once created, much of what happens to that creation can be determined and then controlled by the artist. This is also true for how you go about setting up your life to do more creative work. Artists do not need to ask permission from the art world gurus to work, and they also do not need to ask permission to show their work, or to preserve their work for future generations of viewers.

Placing our work on the Internet is one way to record your art, but it is a reproduction, not the original thing. Besides, there are billions of web sites now, all fighting for their "15 minutes of fame." I prefer to offer the original item-- to put it out there and to keep it out there.

Make the best art you can, and if you really think it's that good, then don't treat it as if it was something that could be picked up at the craft store for a few bucks. Instead, treat it as a "Picasso" worth a million dollars. If you give your own art respect, then perhaps you'll earn more respect from others.

Sample Foundation By-Laws:

BY-LAWS

OF

_____(name)_____ **ART FOUNDATION, INC.**

ARTICLE I
ARTICLES OF ORGANIZATION, CORPORATE SEAL AND FISCAL YEAR

1. Articles of Organization

The name of _____ Art Foundation, Inc. (hereinafter in these By-Laws referred to as the "Foundation"), the location of its principal office and its purposes shall be as set forth in the Articles of Organization and these By-Laws.

The powers of the Foundation and of its trustees, officers, and committees and all matters concerning the conduct and regulation of the affairs of the Foundation and the manner in which, and the officers and agents by whom, its purposes may be accomplished shall be subject to such provisions in regard thereto, if any, as are set forth in the Articles of Organization and these By-Laws. All references in these By-Laws to the Articles of Organization shall be construed to mean the Articles of Organization as from time to time amended.

2. Fiscal Year

The fiscal year of the Corporation shall end on June 30th in each year.

3. Corporate Seal

The Trustees may adopt and alter the seal of the Corporation.

4. Gender

The pronoun "he" or "his", when appropriate, shall be construed to mean also "she" or "her" and the word "chairman" shall be construed to include a female.

5. No Members

The Foundation shall have no members. No person now or hereafter designated by the Foundation as a "member" for any purpose shall be or be deemed to be a member for purposes of the Articles of Organization or the By-Laws of the Foundation or for purposes of Massachusetts General Laws Chapter 180, as amended, or any other law, rule or regulation. Any action or vote required or permitted by Chapter 180 or any other law, rule or regulation to be taken by members shall be taken by action or vote of the same percentage of the trustees of the Foundation.

ARTICLE II
BOARD OF TRUSTEES

1. Election

There shall be a Board of Trustees of not less than two (2) trustees and they shall be those persons named as trustees in the Articles of Organization. The trustees may enlarge the Board and elect new trustees to fill the vacancies caused by such enlargement at any meeting called for that purpose.

2. Vacancies

The remaining trustees for the balance of the term may fill any vacancy on the Board of Trustees. The Board of Trustees shall have and may exercise all the powers of the Board of Trustees notwithstanding any vacancies in their number.

3. Annual and Regular Meetings

The annual meeting of the Board of Trustees shall be held on the third Monday of September in each year, (or on the next business day if that day is a legal holiday) at such time and place as the trustees may determine. In the event the annual meeting is not held on such date, a special meeting in lieu of the annual meeting may be held with all the force and effect of an annual meeting. Regular meetings of the Board of Trustees may be held without call or formal notice at such places and at such times as the Board of Trustees may by notice from time to time determine.

Special meetings of the Board of Trustees may be held at any time and at any place designated in a call by the President or by a majority of the Board of Trustees then in office.

4. Notice of Meetings

Notice of time and place of each meeting of the trustees shall be given to each trustee by mail at least five (5) days or by facsimile, e-mail or other electronic means at least forty-eight (48) hours before the meeting, addressed to him at his usual or last known business or residence address, or in person or by telephone at least twenty-four (24) hours before the meeting.

Notice of all special meetings of the Board of Trustees shall be given to each trustee by the President or the Clerk or, in the case of death, absence, incapacity or refusal of the President and the Clerk, by an officer or the trustees calling the meeting, provided, however, that no notice need be given to any member of the Board of Trustees who is either present or waives notice thereof by a writing which is filed with records of the meeting or who attends the meeting without protesting the insufficiency of notice prior to the meeting or at its commencement. In any case, it shall be deemed sufficient notice to a trustee to send notice by mail, telecopier, or email by delivering such notice to him/her, if by mail at least seventy-two (72) hours before, by mailing it, postage prepaid, addressed to such member at his/ her address as it then appears in the records of the Foundation, or if by telecopier or email at least twenty-four (24) hours before by delivering it to such member at his or her telecopier number or email address as it then appears in the records of the Foundation

5. Powers

The Board of Trustees shall have and may exercise all of the powers of the Foundation, including but not limited to the management and control of its property, the selection and compensation of its Executive Director, if any, the adoption of regulations, the establishment of committees, and the delegation to such persons or committees as the Board of Trustees may deem appropriate of specific powers, duties and authorities.

6. Quorum and Voting

A majority of the Board of Trustees shall constitute a quorum for the transaction of business, but a lesser number may adjourn any meeting from time to time, and the meeting may be held as adjourned without further notice.

When a quorum is present at any meeting, a majority of the trustees present and voting shall decide any question, including election of officers and appointment or election of committees, unless otherwise provided by law, the Articles of Organization, or these By-Laws.

7. Presence Through Communications Equipment

Unless otherwise provided by law or the Articles of Organization or these By-Laws, trustees may participate in a meeting of the trustees by means of a conference telephone or similar communications equipment by means of which all persons participating in the meeting can hear each other at the same time, and participation by such means shall constitute presence in person at a meeting.

8. Action Without Meeting

Any action required or permitted to be taken by the Board of Trustees may be taken without a meeting if all the trustees entitled to vote on the matter consent in writing to the action and such written consents are filed with the records of the Foundation. Such consents shall be treated for all purposes as a vote of the Board of Trustees.

9. Resignations and Removals

Trustees of the Foundation may resign at any time by written notice of resignation filed with the Clerk. Such resignation shall be effective upon receipt unless it is specified to be effective at some later time. Any trustee may be removed from office with or without cause by the affirmative vote of a majority of the trustees then in office.

ARTICLE III
COMMITTEES

1. Executive

The trustees may elect or appoint one or more committees. Members of committees need not be Trustees or Officers of the Corporation. The trustees may delegate to any such committees any or all powers of the Trustees, except those which by law, by the Articles of Organization or by these By-Laws they are prohibited from delegating. Unless the trustees otherwise determine, the Executive Committee (if any) shall have all of the powers of the trustees during intervals between meetings of the trustees, except for the powers specified in Chapter 180 of Massachusetts General Laws.

2. Other Committees

The Board of Trustees may from time to time elect or appoint such committees as they deem necessary or appropriate. The number comprising each committee and the powers conferred upon the same shall be as determined by vote of the Board of Trustees.

3. Conduct of Meeting

Any committee may make rules for the conduct of its business, but unless otherwise provided by vote of the Board of Trustees or in such rules, its business shall be conducted as nearly as may be in the same manner as is provided in these By-Laws for the Board of Trustees.

ARTICLE IV
OFFICERS

1. Enumeration

The officers of the Foundation shall be a President, a Treasurer and a Clerk and such other officers and such agents as the Board of Trustees may in its discretion elect or appoint.

2. Election

The Board of Trustees at its annual meeting or the special meeting in lieu thereof shall elect the President, Treasurer and Clerk. Other officers and such agents as the Board of Trustees may in its discretion elect or appoint may be chosen at such meeting or at any other time. Officers may, but need not be, trustees. So far as is permitted by law, the same person may fill any two or more offices.

3. Term

Except as otherwise provided by law, by the Articles of Organization or by these By-Laws, the President, Treasurer, and Clerk, and such other officers as the Board of Trustees have elected, if any, shall hold office until the next annual meeting of the Board of Trustees until their respective successors shall have been chosen and qualified. Any other officer or agency shall hold office at the pleasure of the Board of Trustees. Any officer may be re-elected to successive terms.

Any officer may resign by notice in writing filed with the Clerk.

4. Vacancies

If any office becomes vacant by reason of death, resignation, removal, disqualification, or otherwise, the Board of Trustees may choose a successor, who shall hold office for the balance of the term.

5. Chairman

If a Chairman of the Board of Trustees is elected, he shall preside at all meetings of trustees at which he is present, except as the trustees shall otherwise determine, and shall have such other powers and duties as may be determined by the trustees.

6. President and Vice President

Unless the trustees otherwise specify, the President of the Corporation shall be the Chief Executive Officer of the Corporation and, subject to the control of the trustees, shall have general charge and supervision of the affairs of the Corporation. The Vice President, if any, shall have all the powers and duties of the President during the absence of the President or in the event of his inability to act. The Vice President, if any, shall have such other duties and powers as the trustees shall determine.

7. Treasurer

The Treasurer shall be the chief fiscal officer of the Foundation. The Treasurer shall have care, custody, collection, and disbursement of the funds, securities and valuable papers of the Foundation, except records and documents required by vote of the Board of Trustees or by these By-Laws to be kept by some other person. Subject to the direction and control of the Board of Trustees, he or she shall have general charge of the financial affairs of the Foundation.

The Treasurer shall, as often as the Board of Trustees shall direct, but at least annually, render a written account of the finances of the Foundation, which account shall become a part of the minutes of the meeting at which it is rendered. The Treasurer shall have power to endorse for deposit or collection all notes, checks, drafts, and other obligations and orders for the payment of money to the Foundation, and shall keep books of account, which shall be at the property of the Foundation and open to inspection at all reasonable times by the Board of Trustees. He or she shall keep the accounts of the Foundation and shall send all notices and conduct all correspondence relating to the financial affairs of the Foundation. If at any time the Treasurer is absent or unable to serve, the Chairman shall have all of the powers given to the Treasurer by these By-Laws.

8. Clerk

The Clerk shall keep a true and accurate record of the meetings of the Board of Trustees in books provided therefor; in the absence of the Clerk from any meeting, a Clerk Pro Tem shall be appointed to keep the minutes thereof. The Clerk shall give or cause to be given and/or published all notices as directed by the President or other officers of the Foundation or the Board of Trustees. He or she shall deliver to the Board of Trustees or the proper officer, as the case may be, any communications received by him or her. All books and records, other than fiscal records, of the Foundation shall be in the custody of the Clerk, including but not limited to the minute books, the Articles of Organization, and an attested copy of these By-Laws with marginal references to all amendments thereto.

9. Other Duties

Each officer shall, subject to the Articles of Organization and these By-Laws, have, in addition to the duties and powers specifically set forth in these By-Laws, such duties and powers as are customarily incident to his/her office and such further duties and powers as the Board of Trustees may from time to time designate.

ARTICLE V
REMOVALS AND VACANCIES

1. Removals

An officer may be removed with or without cause by the vote of a majority of the Trustees. Any officer may be removed for cause only after reasonable notice and opportunity to be heard before the Board of Trustees.

2. Vacancies

The Trustees shall elect a successor if the office of the President, Treasurer or Clerk becomes vacant and may elect a successor if any other office becomes vacant. Each such successor shall hold office for the unexpired term and in the case of the President,

Treasurer and Clerk until his successor is chosen and qualified, or in each case, until he sooner dies, resigns, is removed or becomes disqualified.

ARTICLE VI
DISSOLUTION

Except as may be otherwise required by law, the Foundation may at any time dissolve by vote of the Board of Trustees. In the event of any liquidation, dissolution, termination, or winding-up of the Foundation (whether voluntary, involuntary or by operation of law), all property and assets of the Foundation, personal and real, which shall remain after providing for the payment of its debts and obligations, may be converted into cash and such cash, as well as property not so converted, shall be conveyed, transferred, distributed, and set over outright to such one or more charitable, scientific, or educational institutions or organizations (created and organized for nonprofit purposes similar to those of the Foundation, contributions to which nonprofit institutions or organizations are deductible under Section 170(c) of the Internal Revenue Code of 1984 and which qualify as exempt from income tax under Section 501(c)(3) of said Code, as said sections may, from time to time, be amended or added to or under any successor sections thereto) as two-thirds of the total number of the trustees of the Foundation then entitled to vote may by vote designate and in such proportions and in such manner as may be determined in such vote; provided that the Foundation's property may be applied to charitable, scientific, or educational purposes in accordance with the doctrine of cy pres in all respects as a court having jurisdiction in the premises may direct.

ARTICLE VII
SPONSORS AND OTHER SUPPORTERS OF THE CORPORATION

The Trustees may designate certain persons or groups of persons as sponsors, benefactors, contributors, advisors or friends of the Corporation or such other title as they deem appropriate. Such persons shall serve in an honorary capacity and, except as the Trustees shall otherwise designate, shall have no right to notice of or to vote at any meeting, shall not be considered for purposes of establishing a quorum, and shall have not other rights.

ARTICLE VIII
INDEMNIFICATION

The Foundation shall, to the extent legally permissible and only to the extent that the status of the Foundation as exempt under Section 501(c)(3) of the Internal Revenue Code is not affected thereby, indemnify each of its trustees and officers (including persons who serve at its request as trustee, trustees, and officers of another organization in which it has an interest) against all liabilities and expenses, including amounts paid in satisfaction of judgments, in compromise or as fines and penalties, and counsel fees, reasonably incurred by him/her in connection with the defense or disposition of any action, suit, or other proceeding, whether civil or criminal, in which he/she may be involved or with which he/she may be threatened while in office or thereafter by reason of his/her being or having been such a trustee or officer, except with respect to any matter as to which he/she shall have been adjudicated not to have acted in good faith in the reasonable belief that his/her action was in the best interest of the Foundation; provided, however, that as to any matter disposed of by a compromise payment by such trustee or officer pursuant to a consent decree or otherwise, no indemnification either for said payment or for any other expenses shall be provided unless such compromise shall be approved as in the best interests of the Foundation, after notice that it involves such indemnification, (a) by a disinterested majority of the trustees then in office or (b) by a majority of the disinterested trustees then in office after the Foundation has received an opinion in writing of independent legal counsel to the effect that such trustee or officer appears to have acted in good faith in the reasonable belief that his/her action was in the best interest of the Foundation. Expenses, including counsel fees, reasonably incurred by any such trustee or officer in connection with the defense or disposition of any such action, suit, or other proceeding may be paid from time to time by the Foundation in advance of the final disposition thereof upon receipt of an undertaking by such individual to repay the amounts so paid to the Foundation if he/she shall be adjudicated to be not entitled to indemnification under Section 6 of Chapter 180 of the General Laws.

The right of indemnification hereby provided shall not be exclusive of, or affect, any other rights to which any trustee or officer may be entitled. Nothing contained herein shall affect any rights to indemnification to which corporate personnel may be entitled by contract or otherwise. As used in this paragraph, the terms "trustee" and "officer" include their respective heirs, executors and administrators, and an "interested" trustee is one against whom in such capacity the proceeding in question or another proceeding on the same or similar grounds is then pending.

ARTICLE IX
EXECUTION OF DOCUMENTS

Except insofar as the Board of Trustees may authorize the execution thereof in some other manner, all deeds, leases, transfers, contracts, bonds, notes, checks, drafts, and other obligations made, accepted, or endorsed by the Foundation shall be signed on behalf of the Foundation by either the Chairman or the Treasurer.

ARTICLE X
MISCELLANEOUS

1. Audit

Provision shall be made by the Board of Trustees for an annual audit of the accounts of the Treasurer, either by a committee of one or by an accountant retained by the Board of Trustees for the purpose of such audit.

ARTICLE XI
TAX EXEMPTION

This Foundation is intended to be an organization of the type described in Section 501(c)(3) of the Internal Revenue Code other than private foundation. All powers of this Foundation shall be exercised only in such manner as will assure the operation of this Foundation exclusively for said charitable, scientific, and educational purposes and to assure that this Foundation shall be exempt from federal income tax and that contributions to it shall be deductible pursuant to Section 170(c) of the Internal Revenue Code and that it shall be classified as an exempt organization other than a private foundation, and all purposes and powers herein shall be interpreted and exercised consistent with this intention.

The income of this Foundation for each taxable year shall be distributed at such time and in such manner as not to subject the Foundation to tax under Section 4942 of the Internal Revenue Code. The Foundation hereby is and shall be prohibited from engaging in the following activities as defined in Section 4941 through 4949 of said Code: any act of self-dealing with failing to distribute income, disqualified persons, retaining any excess business holdings, making any investments in such manner as to jeopardize the carrying-out of any of its exempt purposes, or from taking any taxable expenditures. The provisions of this sub-paragraph 2 shall be inapplicable when and if the Foundation receives from the Internal Revenue Service a ruling that the Foundation is not a "private foundation" within the meaning of Section 509 of the Code, and such provisions shall remain inapplicable so long as such ruling remains in effect.

No part of the net earnings of this Foundation shall inure or be payable to or for the benefit of any individual, and no substantial part of the activities of this Foundation shall be the carrying-on of propaganda or otherwise attempting to influence legislation, and the Foundation shall not participate in, or intervene in (including the publishing or distribution of statements), any political campaign on behalf of a candidate for public office.

ARTICLE XII
AMENDMENTS

Except as otherwise provided by law, by the Articles of Organization, or by these By-Laws, these By-Laws may be altered, amended or repealed, or new By-Laws may be adopted, by an affirmative vote of two-thirds of the trustees of the Foundation voting thereon at any annual meeting or at any special meeting called for the purpose, the notice of which meeting shall specify such intention to alter, amend, or repeal and the subject matter of the proposed alteration, amendment, or repeal of the By-Laws to be effected thereby.

Sample of ARTICLES OF ORGANIZATION (from a Massachusetts filing)

A. TO PROMOTE AND CARRY OUT ALL CHARITABLE AND EDUCATIONAL PURPOSES WITHIN THE MEANING OF SECTION 501(C)(3) OF THE INTERNAL REVENUE CODE OF 1986, AS AMENDED (OR ANY SUCCESSOR PROVISIONS THEREFOR), INCLUDING, BUT NOT LIMITED TO THE PURPOSES MORE PARTICULARLY DESCRIBED BELOW: TO PROMOTE, CONSERVE, PRESERVE AND EXHIBIT THE SCULPTURES AND PIECES OF ART OF _____ Name of Artist _____" FOR THE BENEFIT OF THE PUBLIC; TO EXHIBIT HIS VISUAL ART, AND TO ORGANIZE PERFORMANCES OF HIS WRITTEN AND DESCRIBED WORKS; TO COLLECT, CONSERVE, PRESERVE AND EXHIBIT, ON A TEMPORARY OR PERMANENT BASIS, THE ORIGINAL WORKS OF OTHER ARTISTS AS SUCH WORKS RELATE TO THE WORKS OF _____name of artist_____ AND IN THE CONTEXT OF SUCH RELATIONSHIPS; TO ORGANIZE AND SPONSOR EDUCATIONAL ACTIVITIES RELATED TO HIS ART INCLUDING, BUT NOT LIMITED TO SEMINARS, WORKSHOPS AND PERFORMANCES; TO PROMOTE, SUPPORT, FOSTER AND/OR CONTRIBUTE TO THE ESTABLISHMENT, MAINTENANCE AND OPERATION OF A MUSEUM FOR THE PUBLIC EXHIBITION OF _____name of artist's_____ ART. SO FAR, AND ONLY SO FAR AS THE SAME ARE NECESSARY OR CONVENIENT FOR THE ACCOMPLISHMENT OF ITS ENUMERATED PURPOSES AND OBJECTS, TO HAVE THE POWER TO RECEIVE, HOLD AND ADMINISTER SECURITIES, MONIES AND ANY OTHER ASSETS AND PROPERTY AND TO INVEST, REINVEST AND CHANGE THE INVESTMENT OF THE SAME FROM TIME TO TIME, TO RECEIVE, COLLECT AND DISBURSE INCOME, ISSUES, RENTS AND PROFITS ACCRUING THEREFROM, AND APPLY THE SAME TO THE USES AND PURPOSES FOR WHICH THE CORPORATION IS ORGANIZED; TO TAKE AND HOLD, BY GIFT, GRANT, DEVISE, BEQUEST OR OTHERWISE, REAL AND PERSONAL PROPERTY, OF EVERY DESCRIPTION, WITHOUT LIMITATION OF AMOUNT, AND TO MORTGAGE, CONVEY AND DISPOSE OF SUCH REAL AND PERSONAL PROPERTY OF EVERY DESCRIPTION; TO MAKE DONATIONS OF GIFTS FROM ITS ASSETS, INCOME AND PROPERTY TO ANY INSTITUTION OR INSTITUTIONS OF CHARACTER AND WITH PURPOSES AND OBJECTS SIMILAR TO THE PURPOSES AND OBJECTS FOR WHICH THIS CORPORATION IS ORGANIZED. THE

CORPORATION MAY PURSUE ANY OR ALL OF ITS PURPOSES AND OBJECTS AND EXERCISE ANY OR ALL OF ITS POWERS EITHER WITHIN OR ANYWHERE WITHOUT THE COMMONWEALTH OF MASSACHUSETTS. B. IN FURTHERANCE, BUT NOT IN LIMITATION OF THE FOREGOING PURPOSES, THE CORPORATION SHALL HAVE THE POWER AND AUTHORITY: 1. TO SOLICIT, ACCEPT, HOLD, ADMINISTER AND DISPOSE OF MONEY, SECURITIES, AND REAL AND PERSONAL PROPERTY AND TO TAKE AND RECEIVE BY BEQUEST, DEVISE, GIFT OR BENEFIT OF TRUST ANY PROPERTY OR INTEREST THEREIN, REAL, PERSONAL OR MIXED, WHEREVER LOCATED. 2. TO MAKE GIFTS, DONATIONS AND CONTRIBUTIONS OF THE PROPERTY, REAL, PERSONAL OR MIXED, OF THE CORPORATION, INCLUDING BUT NOT LIMITED TO, MONEY, AND TO CONVEY, ASSIGN, LEASE, LEND OR OTHERWISE TRANSFER, WITH OR WITHOUT CONSIDERATION, ANY SUCH PROPERTY. 3. TO ACQUIRE BY PURCHASE, LEASE, CONCESSION, PERMIT, LICENSE OR IN ANY OTHER MANNER WHATSOEVER, AND TO CONSTRUCT, OWN, HOLD, MAINTAIN, IMPROVE, OPERATE, MANAGE, CONTROL, SELL, CONVEY, MORTGAGE, LEASE, RENT OR OTHERWISE DISPOSE OF LANDS, BOTH IMPROVED AND UNIMPROVED, INDUSTRIAL BUILDINGS, OFFICES, STORES, RESIDENCES AND ANY OTHER STRUCTURES AND REAL ESTATE OF EVERY KIND, NATURE AND DESCRIPTION, AND TO ACQUIRE, BY PURCHASE OR OTHERWISE AND TO HOLD, OWN, USE, PLEDGE, SELL OR OTHERWISE DISPOSE OF, AND DEAL IN AND WITH, ALL KINDS OF PERSONAL AND REAL PROPERTY OF EVERY NATURE AND DESCRIPTION. 4. TO INVEST, REINVEST, AND ADMINISTER THE FUNDS OF THE CORPORATION. 5. TO BORROW MONEY AND FROM TIME TO TIME MAKE, ACCEPT, ENDORSE, EXECUTE AND ISSUE PROMISSORY NOTES, BILLS OF EXCHANGE, BONDS, DEBENTURES AND OBLIGATIONS AND EVIDENCES OF INDEBTEDNESS OF ALL KINDS WHEN AND AS THE SAME MAY BE NECESSARY OR CONVENIENT FOR THE ACCOMPLISHMENT OF THE PURPOSES OF THE CORPORATION OR ANY OF THEM; AND, IF DEEMED ADVISABLE, TO SECURE THE SAME BY MORTGAGE, DEED OF TRUST OR PLEDGE, OR OTHERWISE, OF ANY OR ALL OF THE PROPERTY OF THE CORPORATION. 6. TO ERECT, CONSTRUCT, RECONSTRUCT, REPAIR, REMODEL, ALTER, MAINTAIN AND IMPROVE BUILDINGS OF EVERY DESCRIPTION ON ANY LAND OF THE CORPORATION OR UPON OTHER LANDS. 7. TO INVEST IN,

GUARANTEE THE OBLIGATIONS OF, BECOME SURETY FOR, AND TO OTHERWISE LEND MONEY OR OTHER FINANCIAL ASSISTANCE TO ANY ORGANIZATION, ASSOCIATION OR INSTITUTION FORMED TO FURTHER SIMILAR PURPOSES OF THE CORPORATION. 8. TO COOPERATE WITH, SUPPORT, ASSIST, DEAL WITH AND AVAIL ITSELF OF THE FACILITIES AND PROGRAMS OF FEDERAL, STATE AND LOCAL GOVERNMENT AGENCIES, INCLUDING WITHOUT LIMITATION, THE NATIONAL ENDOWMENT FOR THE ARTS AND THE MASSACHUSETTS ARTS COUNCIL. 9. TO CARRY ON ANY ACTIVITY WHICH THE BOARD OF TRUSTEES, IN ITS DISCRETION, DEEMS CALCULATED, DIRECTLY OR INDIRECTLY, TO FURTHER THE AFORESAID CHARITABLE PURPOSES OF THE CORPORATION, AND TO PERFORM AND DO ANY AND ALL THINGS WHICH THE CORPORATION IS EMPOWERED TO DO, OR ANY PART THEREOF, AS PRINCIPAL, OR AFFILIATED CORPORATIONS, ASSOCIATIONS OR TRUSTS, OR OTHERWISE, AND EITHER ALONE OR IN CONJUNCTION OR COOPERATION WITH OTHER PERSONS, GOVERNMENT BODIES AND ORGANIZATION OF EVERY KIND AND NATURE, AND GENERALLY TO ATTAIN AND FURTHER ANY OF THE PURPOSES HEREIN SET FORTH. 10. AS PRINCIPAL, AGENT, CONTRACT OR OTHERWISE, TO MAKE AND PERFORM ANY CONTRACTS OF ANY KIND AND DESCRIPTION AND TO PERFORM AND DO ANY OTHER NECESSARY, SUITABLE OR PROPER ACTS AND THINGS WHICH ARE NECESSARY OR INCIDENTAL TO OR IN FURTHERANCE OF THE ACCOMPLISHMENT OF ANY ONE OR MORE OF THE PURPOSES HEREIN SET FORTH. TO DO ANY AND ALL OTHER LAWFUL THINGS WHICH MAY BE PERMITTED UNDER SECTION 501(C) (3) OF THE INTERNAL REVENUE CODE OF 1986, AS AMENDED, (HEREINAFTER REFERRED TO AS "THE CODE"), AND WHICH ARE ALSO PERMITTED BY CHAPTER 180 OF THE GENERAL LAWS OF THE COMMONWEALTH OF MASSACHUSETTS, AS ARE NOW IN FORCE OR HEREAFTER AMENDED. CONVERSELY, ANY PURPOSE OR ACTIVITY WHICH IS PROHIBITED EXEMPT ORGANIZATIONS UNDER SAID SECTION SHALL BE DEEMED TO BE INVALID AND UNAUTHORIZED, AND ANY PURPOSE OR ACTIVITY PROHIBITED CORPORATIONS ORGANIZED PURSUANT TO SAID CHAPTER SHALL BE DEEMED INVALID AND UNAUTHORIZED. C. AT ALL TIMES, AND NOTWITHSTANDING MERGER, CONSOLIDATION, REORGANIZATIONS, TERMINATION, DISSOLUTION OR WINDING UP OF THE CORPORATION,

VOLUNTARY OR INVOLUNTARY OR BY OPERATION OF LAW, OR ANY OTHER PROVISION HEREOF: 1. THE CORPORATION SHALL NOT POSSESS OR EXERCISE ANY POWER OR AUTHORITY, WHETHER EXPRESSLY BY INTERPRETATION, OR BY OPERATION OF LAW, THAT WILL OR MIGHT PREVENT IT AT ANY TIME FROM QUALIFYING AND CONTINUING TO QUALIFY AS A CORPORATION DESCRIBED IN SECTION 501(C)(3) OF THE CODE, CONTRIBUTIONS TO WHICH ARE DEDUCTIBLE FOR FEDERAL INCOME TAX PURPOSES AND WHICH ARE ALSO PERMITTED BY CHAPTER 180 OF THE GENERAL LAWS OF THE COMMONWEALTH OF MASSACHUSETTS; NOR SHALL THE CORPORATION ENGAGE DIRECTLY OR INDIRECTLY IN ANY ACTIVITY THAT MIGHT CAUSE THE LOSS OF SUCH QUALIFICATION UNDER SECTION 510(C)(3) OF THE CODE, OR WHICH IS PROHIBITED CORPORATIONS ORGANIZED PURSUANT TO SAID CHAPTER. 2. NO PART OF THE ASSETS OR NET EARNINGS OF THE CORPORATION SHALL BE USED NOR SHALL THE CORPORATION EVER BE ORGANIZED OR OPERATED, FOR PURPOSES THAT ARE NOT EXCLUSIVELY CHARITABLE WITHIN THE MEANING OF SECTION 501(C)(3) OF THE CODE. 3. THE CORPORATION SHALL NEVER BE OPERATED FOR THE PRIMARY PURPOSE OF CARRYING ON A TRADE OR BUSINESS FOR PROFIT. 4. NO SUBSTANTIAL PART, AND, DURING SUCH TIME OR TIMES THAT THE CORPORATION IS A PRIVATE FOUNDATION WITHIN THE MEANING OF SECTION 509 OF THE CODE, NO PART OF THE ACTIVITIES OF THE CORPORATION SHALL CONSIST OF ATTEMPTING TO INFLUENCE LEGISLATION (INCLUDING ACTION BY CONGRESS, ANY STATE LEGISLATURE, ANY LOCAL COUNCIL OR SIMILAR GOVERNING BODY, OR THE PUBLIC · IN REFERENDUM, INITIATIVE, CONSTITUTIONAL AMENDMENT, OR SIMILAR PROCEDURE) THROUGH PROPAGANDA OR OTHERWISE (INCLUDING CONTACTING, OR URGING THE PUBLIC TO CONTACT MEMBERS OF A LEGISLATIVE BODY FOR THE PURPOSE OF PROPOSING, SUPPORTING, OR OPPOSING LEGISLATION), NOR SHALL THE CORPORATION, DIRECTLY OR INDIRECTLY, PARTICIPATE IN OR INTERVENE IN (INCLUDING THE PUBLISHING OR DISTRIBUTION OF STATEMENTS) ANY POLITICAL CAMPAIGN ON BEHALF OF OR IN THE OPPOSITION TO ANY CANDIDATE FOR PUBLIC OFFICE. 5. NO SOLICITATION OF CONTRIBUTIONS TO THE CORPORATION SHALL BE MADE, AND NO GIFT, BEQUEST OR DEVISE TO THE CORPORATION SHALL BE

ACCEPTED, UPON ANY CONDITION OR LIMITATION THAT IN THE OPINION OF THE CORPORATION MAY CAUSE THE CORPORATION TO LOSE ITS FEDERAL INCOME TAX EXEMPTION. 6. PURSUANT TO THE PROHIBITION CONTAINED IN SECTION 501(C)(3) OF THE CODE, NO PART OF THE NET EARNINGS, CURRENT OR ACCUMULATED, OF THE CORPORATION SHALL EVER INURE TO THE BENEFIT OF ANY PRIVATE INDIVIDUAL. 7. NOTWITHSTANDING ANY OTHER PROVISIONS OF THESE ARTICLES, IF AT ANY TIME OR TIMES THE CORPORATION IS A PRIVATE FOUNDATION WITHIN THE MEANING OF SECTION 509 OF THE CODE, THEN DURING SUCH TIME OR TIMES: A. THE CORPORATION SHALL DISTRIBUTE ITS INCOME FOR EACH TAXABLE YEAR AT SUCH TIME AND IN SUCH MANNER AS NOT TO SUBJECT THE CORPORATION TO TAX UNDER SECTION 4942 OF THE CODE. B. THE CORPORATION SHALL NOT ENGAGE IN ANY ACT OF SELF-DEALING, AS DEFINED IN SECTION 4941(D) OF THE CODE. C. THE CORPORATION SHALL NOT RETAIN ANY EXCESS BUSINESS HOLDINGS, AS DEFINED IN SECTION 4943(C) OF THE CODE. D. THE CORPORATION SHALL NOT MAKE ANY INVESTMENT IN SUCH A MANNER AS TO SUBJECT THE CORPORATION TO TAX UNDER SECTION 4944 OF THE CODE. E. THE CORPORATION SHALL NOT MAKE ANY TAXABLE EXPENDITURES AS DEFINED IN SECTION 4945(D) OF THE CODE. ALL REFERENCES CONTAINED IN THESE ARTICLES TO THE INTERNAL REVENUE CODE OF 1953, OR TO "THE CODE", SHALL BE DEEMED TO REFER TO THE INTERNAL REVENUE CODE OF 1986, AS AMENDED, AND THE REGULATIONS ESTABLISHED PURSUANT THERETO, AS THEY NOW EXIST OR AS THEY MAY HEREAFTER BE AMENDED. ANY REFERENCE CONTAINED IN THESE ARTICLES TO A SPECIFIC SECTION OR CHAPTER OF THE CODE SHALL BE DEEMED TO REFER TO SUCH SECTION OR CHAPTER AND THE REGULATION ESTABLISHED PURSUANT THERETO AS THEY NOW EXIST OR AS THEY MAY HEREBY BE AMENDED; AND TO ANY CORRESPONDING PROVISION OF ANY FUTURE UNITED STATES INTERNAL REVENUE LAWS AND ANY REGULATIONS ESTABLISHED PURSUANT THERETO. D. UPON THE TERMINATION, DISSOLUTION, OR WINDING UP OF THE CORPORATION IN ANY MANNER OR FOR ANY REASON, VOLUNTARY OR INVOLUNTARY, ITS ASSETS, IF ANY, REMAINING AFTER THE PAYMENT OR PROVISION FOR PAYMENT OF ALL LIABILITIES OF THE CORPORATION SHALL BE DISTRIBUTED TO, AND ONLY TO, ONE OR MORE ORGANIZATIONS DESCRIBED IN SECTION 501(C)(3) OF THE CODE.

Also by the author:

The Art Studio/Loft Manual
For Ambitious Artists and Creators

Do You Need a Great Art Studio-Loft for Little Money?

For painters, sculptors,
printmakers, photographers.
For dancers, performers,
musicians, filmmakers.
For arts and theater groups
- and anyone who needs
gigantic work – live –
exhibition - performance
space. -and for anyone who is
on a limited budget!

- How to find great studios;
  gold mines and pitfalls.
- How to turn them into
  living/work combos.
- Money matters: how to do it
  cheaply or let others pay.
- Real estate and legal
  issues; zoning, negotiation,
  purchase/lease.
- Construction: how to fix
  them up and save money.
- Design and modify large spaces and make them functional for your
  work and needs.
- Cost cutting measures, tricks, ideas, and hard practical advice.
- Think Big! 2,000 SF or 10,000 SF or more!
- How to make great studio space happen for you.

The first book to give practical solutions for thousands of artists and
creators. Stop renting. Get out of the spare bedroom or garage: if you
need and dream of large studio-lofts, you will need to read this book. Just
one idea can save you hundreds of dollars and hours of your time! Just
one idea may find you the studio of your dreams.

A Must Read For All Studio Users

The Art World Dream
Alternative Strategies for Working Artists

Are You an Ambitious Artist?

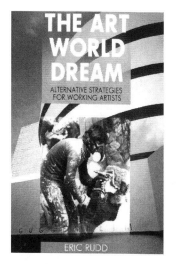

Every artist wants his or her work to hang in the Museum of Modern Art, the Guggenheim, and the Whitney - if not soon, then sometime in the not too distant future. This would signify recognition, financial success and the artist's place in art history.

Whether you are just setting out on a career in art, or have been working for a few years and feel that you can't break free, this book will help you set up your life to allow the art - which you are capable of making - happen. It is not an elementary 'how to paint' or 'how to be an artist' manual. There are plenty of advice books already written for that. That's like giving you advice on how to go hiking in the woods.

You aren't going for a hike; you want to climb Mount Everest! For such an undertaking, there definitely are steps to consider and ways someone can help you. No book can tell you if you will have the strength, but a book can tell you how much strength you will need and how to measure your strength. No book will guarantee that you will be able to raise the funds to finance such an expedition, but a book can tell you what you will probably need and whether there are ways to attain it more easily.

Finally, this book will tell you about other peaks, just as challenging, and present new concepts for you to consider. This book will help you undertake an artistic mission of the most serious nature, needing the utmost determination from you.

Artist Eric Rudd has not only created impressive art that pushes into new technologies, he has also built an incredible infrastructure to do his work. His personal studio complex is inspiring. I would advise other artists to observe what he has done."
Thomas Krens, Director, Solomon R. Guggenheim Museum

A Must-Read for All Serious Artists!